Advertising Annual 2000

Advertising Annual 2000

The International Annual of Advertising
Das internationale Jahrbuch der Werbung
Le répertoire international de la publicité

Publisher and Creative Director: B. Martin Pedersen

Art Director: Massimo Acanfora
Production: Dana Shimizu, Chris Zeller

Editor: Nicole Ray
Associate Editors: Chelsey Johnson, Heinke Jenssen

Published by Graphis Inc.

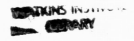

(opposite) Publicis Werbeagentur GmbH *(following page)* Goodby, Silverstein & Partners *(page 6)* Lowe & Partners/SMS

ContentsInhaltSommaire

Remarks: We extend our heartfelt thanks to contributors throughout the world who have made it possible to publish a wide and international spectrum of the best work in the field of design. Entry instructions for all Graphis Books may be requested from: Graphis Inc., 141 Lexington Avenue, New York, NY 10016-8193 or visit our Web site, www.graphis.com

Anmerkungen: Unser Dank gilt den Einsendern aus aller Welt, die es uns durch ihre Beiträge ermöglicht haben, ein breites, internationales Specktrum der besten Arbeiten zu veröffentlichen. Teilnahmebedingungen für die Graphis-Bücher sind erhältlich bei: Graphis Inc., 141 Lexington Avenue, New York, NY 10016-8193. Besuchen Sie uns im World Wide Web, www.graphis.com

Remerciements: Nous remercions les participants du monde entier qui ont rendu possible la publication de cet ouvrage offrant un panorama complet des meilleurs travaux. Les modalités d'inscription peuvent être obtenues auprès de: Graphis Inc., 141 Lexington Avenue, New York, NY 10016-8193. Rendez-nous visite sur notre site web: www.graphis.com

Commentary **Kommentar** Commentaire

You can hurt a Volvo, but you can't hurt it much.

This Volvo was bought new in Ann Arbor, Michigan, in 1959. Its owner paid $2,345 for it, complete. He has raced it, pulled a camping trailer halfway across the country with it, his kids climb all over it, and it's seldom under cover. It has 80,261 miles on it. The hood has never been off, the brakes have never been relined, the original tires lasted 55,000 miles, the clutch hasn't been touched, the valves have never been adjusted (much less ground), and it will still top 95 mph. Total cost of repairs, exclusive of normal maintenance: One hood latch, $4.50. One suspension rod, $10.00. Not all Volvos will do this. But Volvos have a pretty good average. One enthusiastic owner in Wyoming wrote us that he has driven his Volvo over 300,000 miles without major repair. We think he's exaggerating. It's probably closer to 200,000 miles.

Volvo 122S compact. Like the Volvo above, it runs away from other popular-priced compacts in every speed range, yet over 25 miles to the gallon like the 500 economy experts, it actually outdistances.

Drive it like you hate it.

When Volvo came to the U.S. from Sweden in 1956, Chevy was the "hot one," Ford was the "safe one" and Volkswagen was just catching on as the "funny one."

We'd like to say that Volvo immediately caught on as the "tough one." It didn't.

At first only the "car nuts" bought it. They figured that if a Volvo could hold up under Swedish driving (no speed limits), survive Swedish roads (80% unpaved), withstand Swedish winters (30° below), that a Volvo would hold up under anything.

They figured right. Volvos were driven right off showroom floors onto race tracks where they proceeded to win more races of any other compact ever made.

Volvos are still winning races. But that isn't why they're bought today. Volvos are now being used and misused as family cars. They're safe. And on the highway they run away from other popular-priced compacts in every speed range, yet get over 25 miles to the gallon like the little economy cars.

Volvo is now called the "tough one." And it's the biggest-selling imported compact in America today.

You can drive a Volvo like you hate it for as little as $2565.* Cheaper than psychiatry.

A lot of people have the notion that things never wear out on Volvos.
Things wear out on Volvos.
They just wear out a few years later than they do on other cars.

Volvos last an average of eleven years in Sweden where there are no speed limits on the highways, where there are over 70,000 miles of unpaved roads. How long do Volvos last in the States? Volvos have only been here nine years. So nobody really knows yet.

Would you sell your present car to a friend?

Why not? Because it's three or four years old and you figure you've gotten the best years out of it and who knows what's about to go wrong with it?

Volvo owners sell to friends. And they don't lose their friends.

In fact, so many Volvos pass from friend to friend that Volvos are hard to find on used car lots. And when you do find one you pay a good price for it.

I (the writer of this advertisement) bought my Volvo from a friend eight months ago. It was seven years old and had over 100,000 miles on it at the time. It cost about $100 to put it in shape (my friend isn't noted for taking good care of his cars). It needed new brake linings, new king pins, a carburetor overhaul and that's about it. The head has never been off the engine and no major repairs have been made on any other part of the car.

The reason Volvo compacts hold up so well is that Volvos are built in Sweden. In Sweden there are no speed limits on the highways. There are over 70,000 miles of unpaved roads.

In Sweden Volvos are driven hard. Yet they're driven an average of eleven years before people give up on them.

You may not want to keep your Volvo eleven years (although once you get used to not making car payments you might). But wouldn't it be a comfort to own a car that's built well enough to be driven that long?

Especially since you can always sell it to a friend at a good price. With a clear conscience.

Where Ideas Were Weapons, Carl Ally Flourished by Dick Calderhead

"Yeah, well at the Doyle Dane Bernbach agency they tend to goose the consumer. But...... this is Carl Ally, Inc., and at Carl Ally, Inc., we punch them all in the nose."

The advertising business is currently lamenting the fact that "there are no more giants."

What happened? In a business that's spawned such towering greats as Bernbach and Burnett, Ogilvy and Rubicam, Reeves and Harper, plus the scintillating Mary Wells...where did all the giants suddenly go?

They're not developing because America's Ruling Client Class (including virtually all MBAs) have reduced ad people to the status of vendors. How unbelievably demeaning to our business. Carl Ally would have walked out of the office of any client that called him a vendor.

And that's why Carl will never be included in the list of "America's Ten All-Time Most Important Ad People." Carl never wavered from his vision. If that meant resigning accounts that, as he put it, "demeaned his people," so be it. This included even the prestigious IBM, then at the zenith of its corporate power, and a major account for whom they'd done superlative work.

So Carl's agency never reached the critical mass in size or attracted those heavy-spending package goods clients that, through sheer repetition, drive themselves into the public's mind. Leo Burnett's many ubiquitous (and often hopelessly corny) trade figure campaigns rule that roost. Unfortunately, that includes the Marlboro Man.

Carl had a career-long preoccupation with social responsibility. He was famous for saying: "The ultimate client is the consumer." Carl always insisted on relating products to people. Real people.

So Carl wouldn't sell cancer to make a buck. Which meant no high-profile, high-profit cigarette accounts. (30 days after Bill Bernbach died, his agency announced that they would change policy and accept cigarette advertising. RIP, Bill.)

What made Carl so tough, so smart, and so successful for his clients? Carl cut through the crap. (Vendors don't cut through crap; vendors gratefully take whatever they're handed). Read the views of the President of FedEx on this point. Carl cut through the fuzz to help his creative people. (Vendors don't cut through the fuzz; they follow directions.)

Note that Carl started in advertising as a copywriter. Isn't it interesting how many advertising giants (Rubicam, Reeves, Ogilvy, Bernbach, Wells, etc.) began as copywriters. Carl said: "I keep it real simple. I want creative people who write good ads fast the first time, so it gets published and paid for. I don't care what else they do. Anything else they do is their business."

Carl created wealth.

He did it for clients. And he did it for friends. One of his close friends was an ex-Marine fighter pilot who flew combat missions over Guadalcanal. After the war, this fellow hit hard times. Then he hit the bottle. Carl nursed him through rehab, and then helped him launch a magazine that made him wealthy enough to retire in style to Florida.

That's the humane and nurturing side of Carl.

But we're honoring him most for the wealth he created for his clients, using advertising as his weapon. So let's start at the beginning, with Volvo.

Volvo was a sturdy, durable car. But hopelessly out of touch with American car design standards. It was Ally's first account...and what a potential loser he had on his hands. When Carl went to New Jersey to see the cars they'd be selling, accompanied by his two creative partners, Amil Gargano and Jim Durfee, the lame looking sedans that greeted them in the dock area literally had *weeds* growing up through the floorboards.

And they looked like 1947 Fords.

Carl and the boys did some digging, and discovered that the Volvo was a really rugged car that could take incredible punishment. Carl knew he couldn't win on styling or comfort or the traditional sales appeal Detroit relied on. And he certainly couldn't outspend Ford or Chevy. So Carl positioned Volvo as a car so tough it could even survive Swedish winters. So tough, in fact, that the agency sold Volvo on the startling theme: "Drive it like you hate it." (*Hate* it? Can't you just hear the whiney voice of clients you know who'd react to *that* word, associated with their precious product?)

Please remember, if you have doubts about the power of advertising, that absolutely nothing changed except the advertising. And the advertising soon had Volvo back-ordered.

Carl said: "Give me your sick account and I'll make it healthy." When Carl took over on Hertz, they were looking at two sales curves...theirs and Avis's. Avis was coming on like gangbusters...becoming the darling of the business traveler...and was posing a real threat to Hertz's leadership. If the sales curves kept on converging, Avis would one day take over the number one spot from Hertz.

Carl said: "Bullshit!"

Carl was not intimidated by Avis's superb DDB campaign, which had done no less than reinvent the car company. Instead, his advertising punched Avis right in the nose. His ad campaign simply pointed out that Avis was #2 for a reason. They weren't even close to Hertz in size.

The ads made Avis flinch. And they never recovered.

Carl was the spear-carrier. The rainmaker. The downfield blocker. The man with the Vision for his agency.

Yes, Amil Gargano and Jim Durfee were vital to his success. The quality of their work made the campaigns sing. The people they hired kept the work fresh and the quality outstanding. We can't do justice to their role here, as we honor Carl. Perhaps later, in a longer, expanded piece we can pay proper homage to Amil and Jim as Carl's superb original creative team.

But without Carl, the agency would not have been launched. And without Carl, the agency went out of business.

Enough said.

Carl's energy and drive were legendary. He employed not one, but two secretaries. Impatient, Carl once let a secretary go simply because she couldn't dial fast enough to keep up with his urgent stream of phone calls.

Another time, coming back from a client meeting and stuck in traffic in midtown Manhattan, Carl abruptly leapt out of the car and trotted off down the Avenue, leaving his passengers to nurse the car back to the garage. Carl could never sit still watching paint dry.

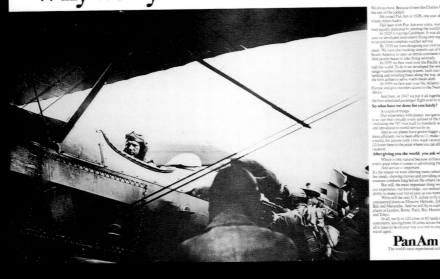

What made Carl so tough?

Carl was a tough-as-nails ex-WWII combat pilot. When you've picked flack out of your flying jacket, you're not going to be intimidated by a client.

Flying was central to Carl's life and to his career. He put himself through the University of Michigan flying crop-dusters. A dangerous way to make a living.

He flew bombers in WWII, and later P-51s and Thunderbolts, two of America's hottest fighters. He was called back for Korea and flew again. (See George Lois's story.) And for the rest of his life, Carl took pleasure in terrifying the hell out of his passengers, who were often his partners and his clients, as well as his friends and family.

But one flying story tops them all.

One night in 1981, as he lined up his Aerostar for a landing at Teeterboro airport, "Wham!" the entire windshield in front of Carl blew out. A sick, disoriented bird had flown into Carl's flight path. The screaming 100-mile-an-hour wind showered Carl's face with shards of broken glass, flying feathers, birdshit and slimy guts. Worst of all, the glass slashed Carl's forehead, and the gushing blood blinded Carl.

The plane veered and bucked as Carl fought to keep the plane level. Carl was on the horn to the Tower, and he didn't lose a beat. "We've taken a bird through the windshield. We're landing and we'll need assistance on the ground."

Since Carl couldn't see, his son Chris (who'd lost an arm in a bike accident) got the wheels down and continued talking Carl in for the landing. "We're heading for the runway…we're about a half mile out…there are the lights…keep straight…we're over the end of the runway…we're coming down OK…." Chris says they landed with hardly a bounce. Carl went to the hospital, got stitched up, and that was that. Always a cool customer under fire.

Important people worked for Carl Ally.

We're talking about some of the creative giants of the industry: Ralph Amiratti, Martin Puris, Ed McCabe, Jim Durfee, Tom Messner and many, many more. Carl, Amil, Jim and this long, long list of superstars created advertising that was inspirational to the entire advertising community. The agency had a macho style and creative quirks all their own.

For instance, Ally often ran very long headlines. An Ally ad for Travelers Insurance that pictured primal men, armed with spears featured this headline: "What Do You Do When the Food You're Looking For Is Also Looking for You?" When Ed McCabe later got his own agency going with Marvin Sloves and Sam Scali, one of his most famous Volvo ads had a three-word headline: "Yes. It flies."

Mike Tesch reminisces over Federal Express. "Carl was able to cut through the bullshit and get right to the point. He always said to me: "Don't decorate the ad." He told Tesch not to fall for adornments…self-conscious addy touches that scream insincerity and frou-frou. Not at Carl's agency, anyway. Carl insisted that his people never camouflage the point of the ad…let it come out big and strong and grab the reader.

"With FedEx, we wanted the readers to identify with the ads. 'Yeah! I'M the underdog. It's MY package won't get there on time. I'M the guy who will get fired. I CAN'T RELY ON ANYONE." Until FedEx.

The killer line that defined the new category leader said it all: "When it absolutely positively has to be there overnight." It's a long

"The creative process is one of exploration, trying to find out what the optimum possibilities are. Why not go out where people are using the product? Drive it or sleep on it… or stick it up your nose if that's where it goes.

In the end, the creative process is one where somebody makes up their mind what they think is right. And if they're right, and if they're good, and they can make somebody else believe what they believe, then you've done it."

slogan…but listen to the cadence and the power of the promise. Tesch did the Fast Talking Man spot…as memorable a commercial as you can name. He also did the infamous Post Office spot…showing a fly-specky, dirty, rude, public-be-damned postal bureaucracy. It was a spot every American related to. We'd been in a post office just like it.

During the life of the campaign, Ally's agency created some 60 spots. They'd fly down to Memphis and sell 10 or 12 out of maybe 15 boards. FedEx was a client from Heaven…the exact opposite of those conflicted, slaughterhouse clients where creative is a barely tolerated afterthought. Ally said: "We don't demean our people or force them to do mediocre work."

The best way to know Carl is to read his own words. Then you decide whether Carl Ally was an edgy, thrill-seeking risk-taker or a brilliant, conscientious, tough-minded intellectual, working in a business that's notorious for surfacy smarts, but underneath, is all too often peopled by hucksters looking for fast ways to make a buck.

Carl said: "Throughout the world I've had the same experience: perhaps 5 percent of all advertising is credible and stimulating, 15 percent is fairly good, another 20 percent is indifferent and the rest is rotten. It's the same everywhere; here, France, Germany, England. But why should advertising be 100% exceptional, when nothing else is? Since Ally's ad campaigns somehow always ended up in the upper tiers of terrific, his standards were exceptionally high.

On teamwork in the agency: "A good account executive gets creative people to like to work for him. I don't know how you legislate that or how you train people. Some guys can go into the creative department and everyone will break their necks to do it…another, with all his homework done, all organized—but they don't want to do it for him. I don't know what it is…but if he has to push creative people—it's a problem."

On creative people doing their own thinking: "Fashion-conscious New York women believe 'You can't be too rich or too thin.' The same is true of information. The problem is a lot of information is useless. Clients and agencies generate tons of it that's often not to the point. So as a creative person, I got my own. I know what I want…I usually have a notion what I'm going to do anyway. All

"Throughout the world I've had the same experience: perhaps 5 percent of all advertising is credible and stimulating, 15 percent is fairly good, another 20 percent is indifferent and the rest is rotten."

"So as a creative person… I usually have a notion what I'm going to do anyway. All I'm looking for is something to reinforce it so when people argue with me, I can shove it back in their faces."

Old Bushmills Irish Whiskey can do anything, any time, any place.

If you want to know what goes into these holiday drinks besides Old Bushmills (yes, even the pink frothy one is a holiday drink—yes, it is made with whiskey), write to us. We'll send you the recipes.

If we missed your favorite holiday drink, make it with Old Bushmills anyway, then send us your recipe. We plan to do this again next year and we don't want to miss a favorite just because we don't know about it. And we

don't want you to miss Old Bushmills just because you don't know about it. Old Bushmills has burnished Scotch flavor without burnished Scotch smokiness—blended whiskey smoothness without blended whiskey blandness.

And if you're wondering why that whiskey straight, Whiskey Sour, Manhattan, Old Fashioned, whiskey on the rocks, and Irish Coffee are in the picture—well, as we said, Old Bushmills can do anything, any time, any place.

9 YEAR OLD BLENDED IRISH WHISKEY · 86 PROOF · BOTTLED IN IRELAND **QUALITY IMPORTERS INC., 55 FIFTH AVE., NEW YORK 3, N. Y.**

I'm looking for is something to reinforce it so when people argue with me, I can shove it back in their faces. Why sit in an office waiting for assorted memos? The creative process is one of exploration, trying to find out what the optimum possibilities are. Why not go out where people are using the product? Drive it or sleep on it…or stick it up your nose if that's where it goes. Come to some conclusions of your own. In the end, the creative process is one where somebody makes up their mind what they think is right. And if they're right, and if they're good, and they can make somebody else believe what they believe, then you've done it."

And finally, listen to Carl (a man who knew war first-hand) describe affluency vs. poverty. Carl addresses an essential problem we still face today. "Over three quarters of the world is out there with no cars, poor housing, inadequate food, poor education, no communications, no clothes, no health care, no nothing—except a big long list of grievances. There was a time when we did not have what the rest of the world now wants. Is it impossible to recognize the connection between reasonable human needs and opportunity? We need to direct the creative juices and energies of the have-it-all society to those of crying-need societies. What alternative is there to bringing acceptable minimums of goods and services that make life bearable to the multitudes who now live on the margins?

"I have arrived at a point in life where I believe that the future has to be populist, which means it has to include everybody; it has to be pacifist, because confrontation is extremely destructive; and it has to be minimalist, enough to get the job done, because we cannot give a few people an excess of everything at the expense of everybody else having little or nothing.

"So I commend to you three criteria for running your own business: populism, pacifism and minimalism. A spread of technological knowledge and jobs and infrastructure throughout a world that includes everybody. And a style of accommodating ourselves to each other that avoids confrontation. I think this is a practical matter, not an idealistic matter and not a political matter. It is a way to preserve us."

We join Fred Smith of FedEx in saying, "Carl, we'll miss you." We'll miss the boundless energy. Your respect for the consumer, and your ferociously high creative standards.

We doubt we'll see the likes of you in our business any time soon.

Fredrick W. Smith *is the Chairman and Chief Executive Officer of the FDX Corporation.*

On the streets of every major city in the world today, the FedEx logo is a major presence. Our name has become a verb meaning to ship something fast and reliably.

While tens of thousands of people have created this enterprise, among the handful whose roles were truly decisive was Carl Ally.

Carl, working with Vince Fagan, FedEx's original head of marketing, created an awareness of the fledgling company through brilliant advertising so successful that the campaigns are still studied today.

Carl's unique blend of incisive observation, communication skills, and passion were instrumental in making the young company prosper and setting the stage for its future dominance of the modern express industry.

I've been privileged to know a few people whom I would describe with the word "genius." Carl Ally is clearly among them. The many pleasurable hours of debate and brainstorming and good fellowship with him are among my fondest business memories. Carl could, better than anyone I have ever known, "cut to the quick." His agency revolutionized advertising, creating an entire new advertising genre. Without him, I'm very sure there would be no Federal Express as we know it today.

Carl was a great colleague, a wonderful friend, and an all around good guy. All of us who knew him well will miss him.

George Lois, *the father of the "Big Idea," is responsible for some of the most memorable campaigns in advertising history.*

My Greco Turkish Love Affair: Pasha Carl Ally was beating the Madison Avenue bushes.

Carl lacked a job and was a model candidate for the Papert Koenig Lois scene in 1961. After a spectacular first year, PKL was proving to be the second most creative agency in all the world: talented, aggressive, brash.

At Campbell-Ewald, Detroit, they made him a troubleshooter and sent him to be a new business specialist in their New York office. Then something went sour and Ally was canned.

The Turk walked the streets for a year.

It got so bad they turned off the lights at home, disconnected his phone. As he walked around and saw everybody, he felt the whole town was looking down their noses at him.

Ad Age described Ally as a person with the humility of a professional lion tamer. But with enemies like Ally's, he was made for our agency.

And it's not an everyday event when someone comes for a job interview with a Turkish bellybutton peeping out of his shirt. When I first met Carl during his interview with Julian Koenig, we asked a few pointed questions about his past. We needed a hotshot to handle Xerox and *The New York Herald Tribune* and we wanted to be sure that what we had heard about him was true. Quick-tempered, boiling with energy and a rat-a-tat talker, Ally shot back, "Fuck you, I don't need this horseshit."

I told Julian, I love him, let's hire this guy fast.

The fat Turk joined us as a VP and account supervisor. Also as PKL's pilot.

He was a pilot in WWII and was called back to fly jets in Korea. I immediately connected with him because I was a ground soldier in Korea when he was flying sorties, attacking Charlie in North Korea. (When I told Carl we G.I.s used to count our jets flying north, and bet each other on how many would get back safely, he almost threw up.)

Xerox was located in Rochester; so Carl shuttled between New York and Rochester in our Beechcraft Bonanza. The plane was a four-seater and I wondered more than once how I ended up at six thousand feet in choppy weather with my life in the hands of a Turk. But I decided a Greek's chauffeur should be a Turk.

On one of our trips to Xerox the plane bounced through a murderous front. My chauffeur looked confident enough behind the controls, but Carl was overweight and smoked a lot. I wondered what would happen if he ever had a heart attack in the air. "Does a Turk ever crap out at the controls?" I asked him.

He smiled Turkishly and said, "Only when a Greek prick who can't fly is his co-pilot." We swooped out of the thick clouds, landed safely, waded through the snow and grabbed a cab to the

It got so bad they turned off the lights at home, disconnected his phone. As he walked around and saw everybody, he felt the whole town was looking down their noses at him.

bile-green buildings of downtown Rochester, where we showed Joe Wilson how to make the Xerox copier famous overnight, and make him and his stockholders rich.

Carl was the most enthusiastic account guy who ever hit Manhattan. Bright, hard-working, passionate. The greatest ad lover in the history of advertising. He knew a great campaign when he saw one, and didn't need any help to sell it.

After we became the first ad agency to go public, I wanted to give Carl a piece of the PKL action. But some of us had become arrogantly respectable and I ran up against a brick wall by suggesting that we make a stockholder of a brash guy with flapping shirttails.

Carl began to feel he was getting the shaft.

Late one night he asked me what was going on, yes or no, and if no, why not? He was slightly tanked and I was hopeful that I could still swing it. I told him it was still being considered, but Ally called me a lying son-of-a-bitch and swung at me in a seething rage. I grabbed the lovable Turk and we wrestled full-out for a scary minute. And then hugged each other with tears in our eyes.

Shortly after that the ad manager of Peugeot moved to Volvo and asked us to take over his three-million-dollar account. This meant we would have to dump Peugeot, a much smaller account, but as out charter client, they helped us pay our bills when we hung out our shingle, and we felt fiercely loyal and grateful to them for giving us our start. We stuck with Peugeot and told Carl to take Volvo and start his own agency if that's what he wanted. He did. When he left PKL to start Carl Ally Inc., never was a Greek more shook up by the flight of a Turk.

My affection for him endures to this day.

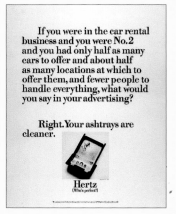

Mack Hanan *is a management consultant. He was present at the inception of Carl Ally's first agency.*

When I introduced Carl Ally to Volvo, I kept both hands in my pockets as much as possible so my white knuckles might not show. An irresistible force was to confront a hard-to-move object, the stolid Swedes.

With small budgets and even smaller shares of mind and market, Volvo needed iconoclastic advertising. Yet the Swedes regarded Volvo—ridiculed in the United States as a born-again 1939 Ford—as an icon. In Sweden, it was sold with a lifetime guarantee. Carl's vision was simple: look past or look through the outside, bring the insides out.

Over the weekend, he borrowed a dealer's loaner. Up and back, he plowed a muddy, woodsy field with it. When the outsides were hard to see, he crouched a photographer behind a rocky outcrop and shot the car, partially airborne, charging into space. He headlined it: "Drive This Car Like You Hate It."

The Swedes looked at the ad. As far as I remember, it was the only one Carl showed. They looked at each of us. Hate their icon? Bury it in mud? Show it without the country club in the background?

"Who would be attracted by this advertising?" the president asked Carl.

"Drivers. Car drivers. People who love driving cars. Precision-engineered cars. Cars that chew up the road. Cars that chew up other cars. Cars that show up other drivers. Cars that people can't wait to drive and never want to stop."

"But we have preferred a different market," the president said. Professional people; doctors, lawyers, scientists. "Do we really want your kind of people?" he asked Carl.

"Everyone we can get," Carl said.

"And this advertising will get them?"

"Everyone we can get," Carl said.

"How many of them will spend their dollars with us?" the president asked.

"Everyone we can get," Carl said.

Carl and I drove away in his loaner, cleaned up for the occasion. He had his first account for Carl Ally, Inc. I asked him how many other accounts he wanted for the new agency. "Everyone we can get," Carl said.

Direct Response.

Freude am Fahren

Joy-stick.

Freude am Fahren

Heaven on Earth.

Freude am Fahren

Agency: BBDO Düsseldorf
GmbH Advertising
Creative Director:
Michael Osche
Art Director: Morris Aberham
Copywriter: Arno Haus
Photographer: René Jaschke
Client: BMW AG, Munich

Déjà vw.

Some experiences are just too good to only have once.

So we brought it back. The new Beetle from Volkswagen.

Take one for a test drive and we think you'll agree...

Some experiences are just too good to only have once.

So we brought it back. The new Beetle from Volkswagen.

Take one for a test drive and we think you'll agree...

Some experiences are just too good to only have once.

Visit Southern States Volkswagen. 2421 Wake Forest Road. (919)828-0901.

Volkswagain.

Remember everything you heard about the new Volkswagen Beetle in the '50's?

This time it's even better. See for yourself at Southern States Volkswagen. 2421 Wake Forest Road. (919)828-0901.

Remember everything you heard about the new Volkswagen Beetle in the '60's?

This time it's even better. See for yourself at Southern States Volkswagen. 2421 Wake Forest Road. (919)828-0901.

Remember everything you heard about the new Volkswagen Beetle in the '70's?

This time it's even better. See for yourself at Southern States Volkswagen. 2421 Wake Forest Road. (919)828-0901.

this page)
Agency: Goodby, Silverstein
& Partners
Creative Directors,
Art Directors: Jeffrey Goodby,
Rich Silverstein
Copywriter: Jim Haven
Photographer: Michael Klein
Client: Porsche

(opposite, top)
Agency: Goodby, Silverstein
& Partners
Creative Directors,
Art Directors: Jeffrey Goodby,
Rich Silverstein
Copywriter: Jeffrey Goodby
Photographer: Michael Klein
Client: Porsche

(opposite, bottom)
Agency: Goodby, Silverstein
& Partners
Creative Directors,
Art Directors: Jeffrey Goodby,
Rich Silverstein
Copywriter: Jim Haven
Photographer: Vic Huber
Client: Porsche

Introducing the new 911. Its true eloquence can only be expressed on the open road. With a 296 horsepower water-cooled engine and 35 years worth of wisdom. Once again the 911 evades description, moving us to say: Porsche. There is no substitute."

**1.1 million words in the English language
and not one can describe the feeling.**

PORSCHE

35 years after the first, we unveil the next. Water cooled. 296 horsepower. And the collective knowledge of five generations of Porsche engineers, gathered in one place. The new 911. Porsche. There is no substitute."

Pictured above:

Everything we know so far.

The privileges of adulthood are as follows: 296 water-cooled horses. Zero to 60 in 5.2 seconds. And the ability to summon adrenaline with the turn of a key. The new 911 is here. Contact us at 1-800-PORSCHE or www.porsche.com and see once again: Porsche. There is no substitute."

Youth is much better when you're old enough to enjoy it.

THINGS TO DO:

PICK UP LAUNDRY

BUY GROCERIES

SAVE WORLD

THE ELECTRIC CAR IS HERE.

1.800.25ELECTRIC or www.gmev.com

THE ANSWER TO L.A.'S SMOG PROBLEM.

ANOTHER CAR.

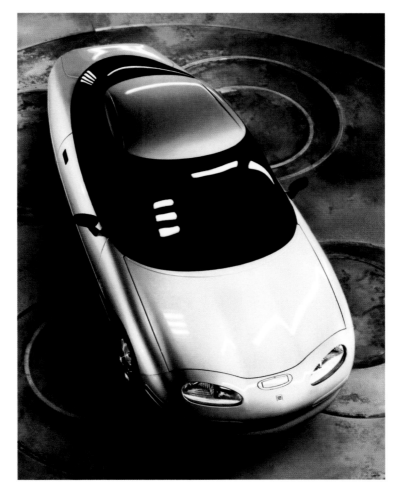

THE ELECTRIC CAR IS HERE.

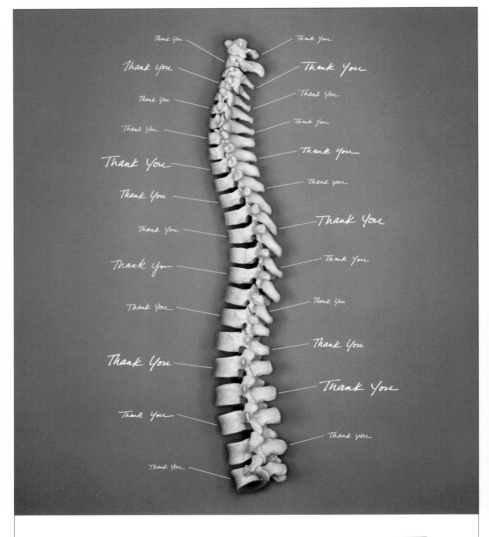

The RX 300. It rides a whole lot smoother than other SUVs. A fact that you and each of your 24 vertebrae will certainly appreciate.

THE RELENTLESS PURSUIT OF PERFECTION.

Go places mere mortals will never see.

Unless they have a quarter. The V8-powered LX 470.

"I yam what I yam," said the ES 300's
new, more powerful VVT-i engine.

LEXUS
THE RELENTLESS PURSUIT OF PERFECTION.

The RX 300. As rugged as any other SUV on the block. It just rides a whole lot smoother. **THE RELENTLESS PURSUIT OF PERFECTION.** **LEXUS**

Ahhh, life at the top. Where the air is incredibly thin. The V8-powered LX 470. **THE RELENTLESS PURSUIT OF PERFECTION.** **LEXUS**

Us.   Them.

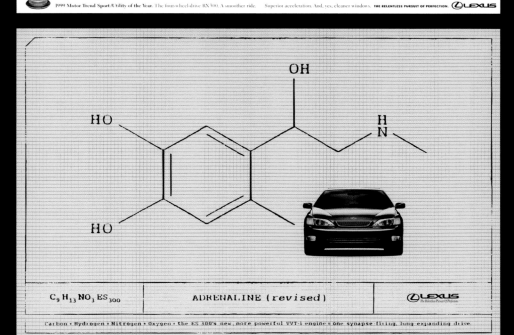

$C_9 H_{13} NO_3 ES_{300}$ ADRENALINE (revised)   ⨷LEXUS

Carbon • Hydrogen • Nitrogen • Oxygen • the ES 300's new, more powerful VVT-i engine = one synapse-firing, lung-expanding drive.

Trees have tree-huggers. Hips have hip-huggers.
Curves have the ES 300's new Vehicle Skid Control.

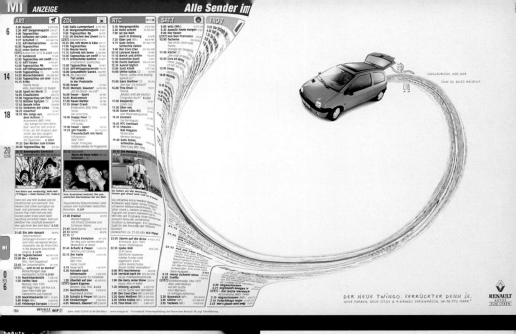

UNGLAUBLICH, WAS DER TWINGO SO ALLES REINTUT.

DER NEUE TWINGO. VERRÜCKTER DENN JE.
NEUE FARBEN, NEUE SITZE & 4 AIRBAGS SERIENMÄSSIG. AB 96.950 MARK.*

RENAULT
AUTOS ZUM LEBEN

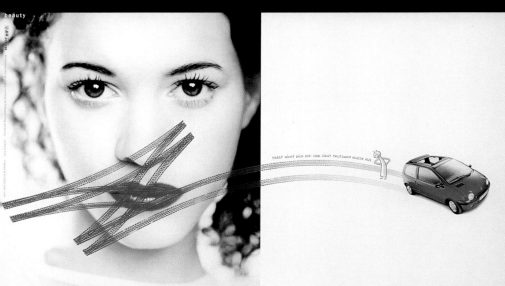

beauty

TRÄGT NICHT DICK AUF. UND SIEHT TROTZDEM KLASSE AUS.

DER NEUE LOOK

DER NEUE TWINGO. VERRÜCKTER DENN JE.
NEUE FARBEN, NEUE SITZE & 4 AIRBAGS SERIENMÄSSIG. AB 96.950 MARK.*

RENAULT
AUTOS ZUM LEBEN

SONDERSITZUNG sonderlich dringend einberufen und sonderlich lang

PARLAMENT

Krise in Bonn

Erneut Streit über den Umzug nach Berlin.
Wer soll den Bundesadler transportieren?

Bonns letzter Umzugskarton war ordnungsgemäß gepackt, beschaftet und verladen — ein wahrhaft bewegender Moment in der Geschichte des Parlaments. Doch siehe da, im Plenarsaal hatte man doch tatsächlich etwas vergessen.

Bemerkt wurde der Vogel von Hausmeister I. N. Ordnung, der für sein Adleraugen bekannt und für die Geschichte bestätigen. Kann er sicher das Ihre augefallt Und sei und überhaupt Der Zigarreten $ 8,093

Wie im Fluge verbreitete sich der dringende Nachricht auf den Gängen und im Foyer. Sofort wurde eine sonderlich Einschätzung der Lage. War doch

für jeden im Saale offensichtlich, daß die „lette Henne", wie die Volksvertreter lobevoll ihren Vogel nennen, ob der scheren Größe in keine der Versöhnt wurde in den neuen, europormenten Umzugskisten passen würde.

So verwundert es nicht, daß die Pragmatiker vorschlugen, einfach alle Flügel radikal zu stutzen. Nicht gerade zur Freude der zahlreich anwesenden Vogelschützer.

Haushaltsexperten dagegen sprachen sich erhitzt für das Einschmelzen und die anschließende Veräußerung aus. Eine Fraktion, aus Sicht der Reclam-Leser-Fraktion, die im lautstarken Zwischenrufen zu Vernünft wurde sie end durch den beschwingte Vortrag von Horst Adler, der seine Rede durchweg mit Zitaten des mittelhochdeutschen

Lynikers Walther von der Vogelweide unterfütterte. „Das schießt doch den Vogel ab", kommentierte der „Ultra" Habicht von Greifswald der Ausführungen seines Vorredners und gipfelte in der Forderung „jeder muß irgenwann, irgendwo und irgendwie mal Federn lassen". Was dann geschah, überraschte sogar altengesessene „Spaßer" in Bonn. Überall wurden Anträge formuliert, diskutiert, umformuliert, diskutiert, neu formuliert und ohne langes Federlesen eingebracht.

Zur Abstimmung kam es an den Tage nicht mehr, auch nicht am nächsten und den daraufolgenden. Eigentlich verrückt, und uneigentlich, fragt sich der Leser.

MICHAEL KÖCHER

DER INNENRAUMKÜNSTLER EMPFIEHLT. MEHR OFFENHEIT FÜR JEDEN UNFUG.

DER NEUE TWINGO. VERRÜCKTER DENN JE.
NEUE FARBEN, NEUE SITZE & 4 AIRBAGS SERIENMÄSSIG. AB 96.950 MARK.*

RENAULT
AUTOS ZUM LEBEN

27

Why should a smooth ride be confined to smooth surfaces? With Audi's four-link front suspension you'll feel like detouring down a country road with your foot off the brake pedal.

A   B

Slide your finger from point A to point B.

That's how smooth a ride in an Audi feels. The Audi A4. Drive it.

Audi

Advancement through Technology

SAAB

(opposite)
Agency:
The Martin
Agency
Creative
Directors:
Kerry
Feuerman,
Rob
Schapiro
Art Director:
Christopher
Gyorgy
Copywriter:
Chris
Jacobs
Photographer:
George
Contorakes
Client:
Saab Cars
USA, Inc.

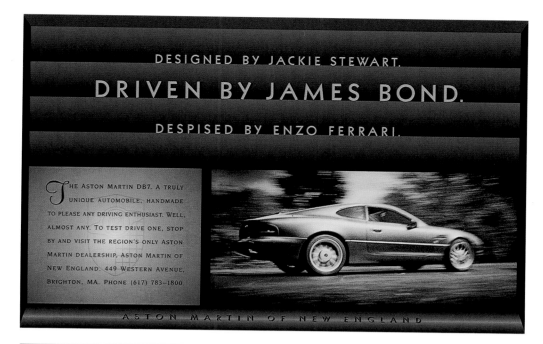

DESIGNED BY JACKIE STEWART.

DRIVEN BY JAMES BOND.

DESPISED BY ENZO FERRARI.

The Aston Martin DB7. A truly unique automobile, handmade to please any driving enthusiast. Well, almost any. To test drive one, stop by and visit the region's only Aston Martin dealership, Aston Martin of New England. 449 Western Avenue, Brighton, MA. Phone (617) 783-1800.

ASTON MARTIN OF NEW ENGLAND

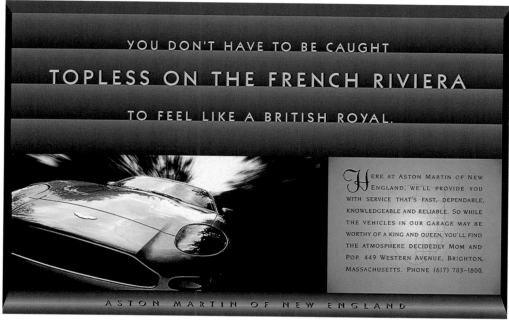

YOU DON'T HAVE TO BE CAUGHT

TOPLESS ON THE FRENCH RIVIERA

TO FEEL LIKE A BRITISH ROYAL.

Here at Aston Martin of New England, we'll provide you with service that's fast, dependable, knowledgeable and reliable. So while the vehicles in our garage may be worthy of a king and queen, you'll find the atmosphere decidedly Mom and Pop. 449 Western Avenue, Brighton, Massachusetts. Phone (617) 783-1800.

ASTON MARTIN OF NEW ENGLAND

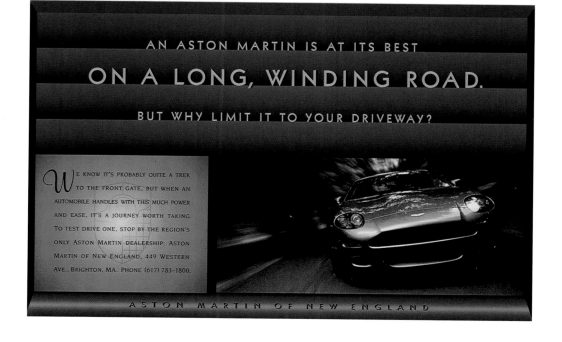

AN ASTON MARTIN IS AT ITS BEST

ON A LONG, WINDING ROAD.

BUT WHY LIMIT IT TO YOUR DRIVEWAY?

We know it's probably quite a trek to the front gate, but when an automobile handles with this much power and ease, it's a journey worth taking. To test drive one, stop by the region's only Aston Martin dealership: Aston Martin of New England, 449 Western Ave., Brighton, MA. Phone (617) 783-1800.

ASTON MARTIN OF NEW ENGLAND

(this page)
Agency:
Ingalls
Creative
Directors:
Rob Rich,
Steve
Bautista
Art Director:
Sean
Farrell
Copywriter:
Chris
DeCarlo
Photographer:
Jim Flynn
Client:
Aston Martin

Agency: Goodby, Silverstein & Partners
Creative Directors:
Jeffrey Goodby, Rich Silverstein
Art Director: Karin Onsager-Birch
Copywriter: Jeff Huggins
Photographer: Michael Rausch
Client: American Isuzu Motors Inc.

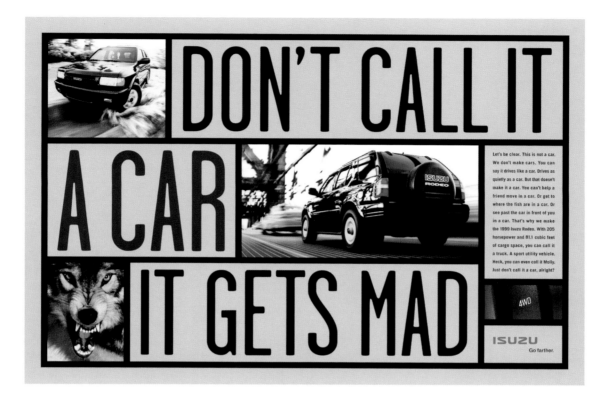

Creative Directors: Bruce Bildsten,
Tom Lichtenheld
Art Director: Steve Driggs
Copywriter: Mike Gibbs
Client: BMW of North America

(opposite, top right, bottom left)
Agency: Fallon McElligott
Creative Directors: Bruce Bildsten,
Tom Lichtenheld
Art Director: Steve Sage
Copywriter: Riley Kane
Photographer: Michael Rausch
Client: BMW of North America

...es **the driver** loves **the car** loves **the road** loves **the driver** loves **the car** loves **the road** loves **the driver** loves **the car** loves **the road** loves **the driver** loves **the ca**

Caress.

The road teases. The foot presses the accelerator. The engine breaks into song. The tires embrace the tarmac,

while the steering wheel assumes the role of dance partner, joyfully following your lead. From its near perfect

balance, to the precise response of every control, no other car is as perfectly attuned to you as a BMW.

The Ultimate Driving Machine

Hug.

Now with more room for little white arrows.

Kiss.

Luxury with a strong jolt of adrenaline. The new 7 Series is the exception to the belief that a luxury car need be uninspired and boring. This is an unequivocally spacious, luxurious and safe car. Yet, once behind the wheel you become entranced by an automobile that is bold. Invigorating. Even daring. This is the 7 Series. It is not your common luxury car. It is, however, the prescribed cure for one.

The Ultimate Driving Machine®

Unexpectedly playful. Thoroughly protective. Is this the ultimate automotive paradox? We believe exhilarating performance is the greatest luxury a car can provide. Witness the new 7 Series. It excites the senses, without abandoning common sense. By surrounding you with the most sophisticated safety features. Making it a thrilling choice for those seeking a practical car. And a practical choice for those seeking a thrilling car.

The Ultimate Driving Machine®

A powerful retort to the statement "You're only young once." There is a fountain of youth, and it has been cleverly disguised as the new 7 Series. This is an automobile whose performance is not validated by statistics, but by how utterly alive it makes you feel. It has the rare ability to thrill you. Exhilarate you. Rejuvenate you. While protecting you. Making each day feel like an extended recess.

The Ultimate Driving Machine®

(opposite)
Agency: Fallon McElligott
Creative Directors:
Bruce Bildsten,
Tom Lichtenheld
Art Director:
Steve Sage
Copywriter: Tom Rosen
Photographer: Graham
Westmoreland
Client: BMW of North
America

(this page)
Agency: Fallon
McElligott
Art Director: Steve Sage
Copywriter: Tom Rosen
Client: BMW
of North America

The new M5. Coming soon.

(this page)
Agency: Bozell Worldwide
Creative Director:
Ken Sakoda
Art Director: John Zegowitz
Copywriter: Chris Brown
Photographer: William Hawkes
Client: Kawasaki Motors
Corp., USA

(opposite)
Agency: Weber, Hodel, Schmid,
Creative Directors:
Liliane Lerch,
Book Creative Directors:
Peter Ruch, Beda Achermann
Art Director: Jürg Aemmer
Book Art Director:
Markus Bucher
Copywriter: Natascha Posch
Illustrator: Sandro Fabbri
Campaign Photographer:
Peter Hebeison
Book Photographers:
Raymond Meier, Max Vadukul,
Urs Möckli, Glen Luchlord
Client: Micro Compact Car
smart GmbH

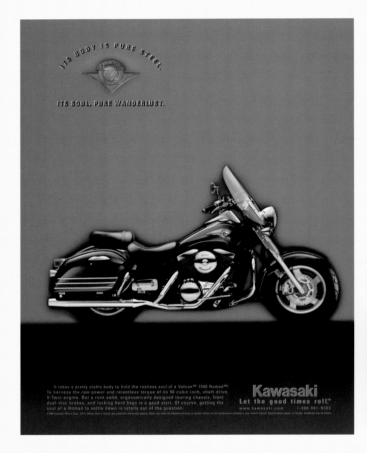

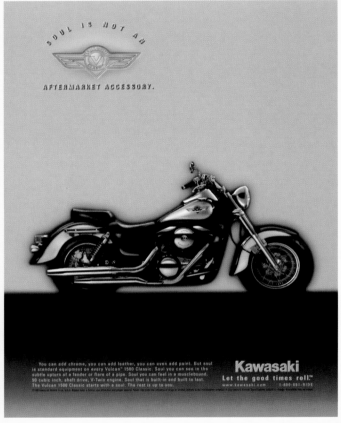

Wie sich der smart für Ihre Sicherheit stark macht, steht im smart Buch. Den smart können Sie ab Juli im smart Center bestellen, das Buch schon jetzt und kostenlos: 01802 2802 (D), 0844 848 400 (CH), 0660 31 2090 (A) oder www.smart.com.

smart reduce to the max.

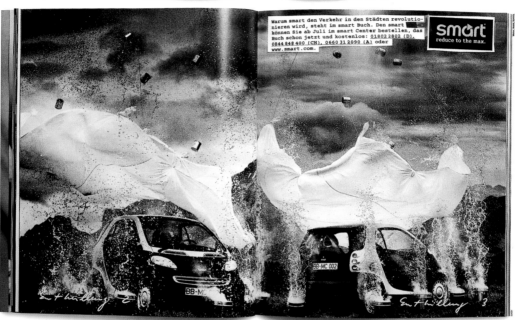

Warum smart den Verkehr in den Städten revolutionieren wird, steht im smart Buch. Den smart können Sie ab Juli im smart Center bestellen, das Buch schon jetzt und kostenlos: 01802 2802 (D), 0844 848 400 (CH), 0660 31 2090 (A) oder www.smart.com.

smart reduce to the max.

Wie in nur einer Stunde aus einem roten ein gelber, ein weißer oder ein schwarzer smart wird, steht im smart Buch. Den smart können Sie ab Juli im smart Center bestellen, das Buch schon jetzt und kostenlos: 01802 2802 (D), 0844 848 400 (CH), 0660 31 2090 (A) oder www.smart.com.

smart reduce to the max.

(this page)
Agency: Hoffman York
Creative Director,
Copywriter: Tom Jordan
Art Director, Designer: Ken Butts
Photographer: Peter Carter
Digital Composition: Jeff Mueller
Client: Jensen

(opposite)
Agency:
Arnold Communications
Creative Director: Ron Lawner
Art Directors:
Alan Pafenbach, Lance Jensen
Client: Volkswagen of America, Inc.

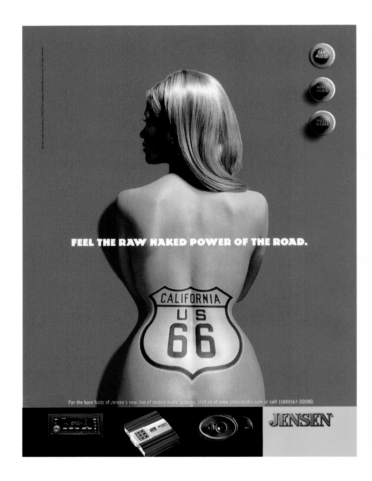

Suddenly the world's glass is half full again.

Drivers wanted. VW

A car like this comes around
only twice in a lifetime.

Drivers wanted. VW

So, anything interesting happen in the last 19 years?

Drivers wanted. VW

The engine's in the front,
but its heart's in the same place.

Drivers wanted. VW

A checking account dedicated to the most dedicated fans in the world.

A checking account dedicated to the most dedicated fans in the world.

What is it about you that
most big banks are interested in?

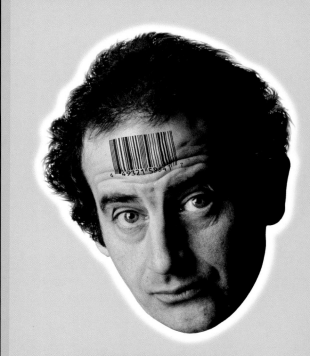

How does your bank recognize you?

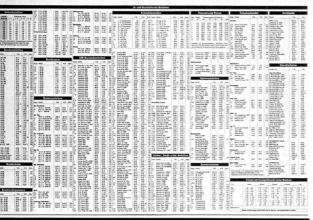

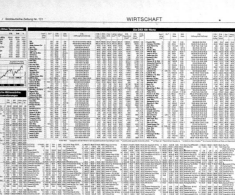

Asset formation abroad.   For reasons of discretion, we would like to reserve the details for a personal meeting.

Appointments on 030/869 869 77

LandesBank
Berlin

International tax-exempt foundations.   For reasons of discretion, we would like to reserve the details for a personal meeting.

Appointments on 030/869 869 77

LandesBank
Berlin

190% allocation of losses.   For reasons of discretion, we would like to reserve the details for a personal meeting.

Appointments on 030/869 869 77

LandesBank
Berlin

(this page)
Agency:
Scholz & Friends,
Berlin
Creative
Directors:
Martin
Pross, Joachim
Schöpfer,
Sebastian Turner
Designer:
Wolfgang Ring
Photographer:
Metthias
Koslik
Client: Landes
Bank Berlin

(opposite, top)
Agency:
The Martin
Agency
Creative
Director:
Cliff Sorah
Art Director:
Jimmy
Ashworth
Copywriter:
Scott Stripling
Photographer:
Darran
Rees
Studio Artist:
Rob Larsen
Print
Producer:
Leslie Rennolds
Client:
Bank One

(opposite, bottom)
Agency:
The Martin
Agency
Creative
Director:
Cliff Sorah, Joe
Alexander
Art Director:
Jimmy Ashworth
Copywriter:
Scott
Stripling
Photographer:
Darren Rees
Studio Artist:
Rob Larsen
Print Producer:
Becky Atkins
Client:
Bank One

Just about everywhere.

More ATMs, more branches, 24hr telebanking & online banking.

1-800-BANK ONE

For whatever's missing, loan by phone.

Answers on home equity loans, before you hang up.

1-800-800-LOAN

Let's recap. That's big, thick hair.

For the record, that's super straight hair.

In case you were wondering, you get real shiny hair.

(this page)
Agency: Saatchi & Saatchi, Vietnam
Client: Head and Shoulders

(opposite, top left)
Agency: BBDO Canada
Creative Directors: Jack Neary,
Michael McLaughlin
Art Director: Michael McLaughlin
Copywriter: Jack Neary
Photographer: Chris Gordaneer
Client: Pepsi–Cola Canada Beverages

(opposite)
Agency: BBDO Canada
Creative Directors: Michael McLaughlin,
Stephen Creet
Art Director: Ken Morgan
Copywriter: Ian MacKellar
Photographer: Philip Rostron
Typographer: John Silva
Client: Pepsi–Cola Canada Beverages

FOREVER YOUNG.

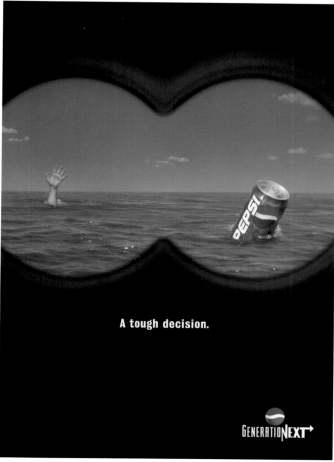

A tough decision.

(this page)
Agency: BL/LB
Creative Director:
Frederique Gadesaude
Photographer:
Hans Neleman
Client: Hennessy

(opposite)
Agency: Hoffman York
Creative Director:
Tom Jordan
Art Director, Designer:
Jerome Marucci
Copywriter:
Mike Herlehy
Client: Barton Brands

WE BRITISH ONLY GET VERBOSE ABOUT SERIOUS THINGS.
LIKE GREAT TASTING ALE.

Usually we're known for being reserved. Circumspect. Even a bit terse. And in general, that is indeed the case. But upon occasion, something comes along that gets us utterly rambunctious. At least by our standards.

The introduction of Tetley's ale to America is such an occasion. Tetley's is as unique an ale as you'll find on either

The secret to Tetley's exceptional taste is its Smoothflow process, which combines the quality of ingredients with a unique nitrogenated gas pressure system. You wouldn't think that so much physics goes into one glass of beer. But it does.

When drawn from a tap, carbon dioxide is kept to a minimum. Added nitrogen gas creates small, compact bubbles. The result is a long-lasting head and smooth taste.

This chemical reaction isn't, however, limited to the tap. When you open a Tetley's can, the release of nitrogen is triggered from an in-can floating device technically known by beer experts as a widget. Once again, a distinctive head forms above a swirl of small bubbles as you pour the creamy, amber ale into your glass.

side of the Atlantic. Its brewing standards are different. Its history is different. Even the composition of something as seemingly trivial as the can is different.

While Tetley's may be new to you, it's certainly no, as you Yanks would say, "spring chicken". Joshua Tetley made his first batch way back in 1822. So while you were starting a country, we were perfecting the taste of ale. We Brits had our priorities, you know.

Today, Tetley's is one of the most popular ales in all of England as more than 1,200 pints are consumed every minute. Which leaves very little time for small talk or any other sort of talk.

The reason? We should tell you right now that there are quite a few. It starts with something called "Smoothflow". This is a process that combines the quality of the brew's ingredients with a unique nitrogenated gas pressure system. What results is a smooth and creamy taste.

Of course, let's not diminish the importance of the ingredients. They include a perfect blend of malted barley, a selected variety of English hops and mineral rich water from deep below the Yorkshire Dales. In addition to all of this, we

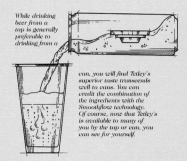

While drinking beer from a tap is generally preferable to drinking from a

can, you will find Tetley's superior taste transcends well to cans. You can credit the combination of the ingredients with the Smoothflow technology. Of course, note that Tetley's is available in many of you by the tap or can, you can see for yourself.

also use yeasts that date back to our very first ale.

To give Tetley's that final bit of individuality, we use "Yorkshire Square" fermenting vessels — a special feature that also dates way back to the early days of brewing Tetley's. As special yeast is added to these square tubs, the brew starts to ferment. Then, the creamy head pushes itself to the upper level, where it can be skimmed without disturbing the brew below. This gives the ale plenty of time to settle, which allows the flavors to mingle and produce a taste of great character.

Tetley's is now available in both draught and cans in Boston, Providence, Philadelphia, Baltimore and northern New Jersey. Or for a much longer trip, you could also go to England.

DRAUGHT
SMOOTHFLOW
TETLEY'S
ENGLISH ALE
ESTD 1822
SMOOTH & CREAMY
YORKSHIRE'S FINEST PUB ALE
14.9 FL OZ (440 ml)

THIS CAN CONTAINS A WIDGET

Before the bartender pours you a glass of Tetley's, make sure he's received the proper training. First, he should tilt the glass at a 45 degree angle. Next, allow the ale to pour down the side of the glass until it comes level with the spout. Then straighten the glass. Once Tetley's has settled, top it off for a full head.

Tetley's™ English Ale, imported from Leeds, England, by Barton Beers, Ltd., Chicago, IL.

ABSOLUT TCHOTCHKE.

(opposite)
Agency: TBWA/Chiat/Day
Creative Director: Geoff Hayes
Art Director,
Copywriter: Scott Carlson

Photographer: Mitch Greenblatt
Client: Absolut Vodka
(top left)
Agency: TBWA/Chiat/Day
Art Directors: Marc Klein,

David Carter
Copywriter: Toby Barlow
Photographer:
Nadav Kander
Client: Absolut Vodka

(top right)
Agency: TBWA/Chiat/Day
Creative Director:
Geoff Hayes
Art Director, Copywriter:

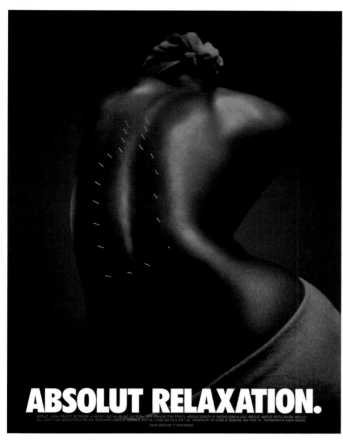

Tom Quaglino
Photographer: Steve Bronstein
Client: Absolut Vodka
bottom left)
Agency: TBWA/Chiat/Day

Creative Director: Geoff Hayes
Art Director: Hajime Ando
Copywriter:
Richard Overall
Illustrator: Leigh Wells

Photographer: Steve Bronstein
Client: Absolut Vodka
(bottom right)
Agency: TBWA/Chiat/Day
Creative Director: Geoff Hayes

Art Director: Dan Braun
Copywriter:
Bart Slomkowski
Photographer: Steve Bronstein
Client: Absolut Vodka

In a past life I was a gypsy. I drank a love potion meant for another and lost my heart to a horse.

In a past life I was pure, glacial spring-water.

In a past life I was a great lover. I left not a heart unbroken in all of Spain or France, or Italy. But Greece, ahh, my apologies to the ladies of Greece. A man does not stay eighteen forever.

In a past life I was pure, glacial spring-water.

In a past life I was an Egyptian Queen. I know how the pyramids were built and exactly what they mean. But I'm not talking.

In a past life I was pure, glacial spring-water.

(opposite page, top, bottom)
Agency: The Martin Agency
Creative Directors:
Mike Hughes,
Jamie Mahoney
Art Director: Jamie Mahoney
Copywriter: Raymond
McKinney
Photographers:
Nadav Kander, Hashi
Print Producer: Linda Locks
Client: Finlandia Vodka

(opposite page, middle)
Agency: The Martin Agency
Creative Directors:
Mike Hughes,
Jamie Mahoney
Art Director: Jamie Mahoney
Copywriter: Raymond
McKinney
Photographers:
Jim Erickson, Hashi
Print Producer: Linda Locks
Client: Finlandia Vodka

(this page)
Agency: Clarity Coverdale Fury
Creative Director,
Art Director: Jac Coverdale
Copywriter: Jerry Fury
Photographer: Raymond Meeks
Client: Belvedere Vodka

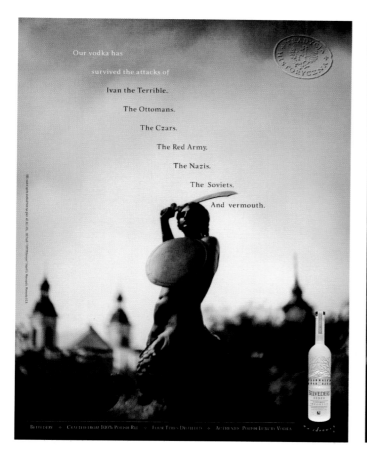

Agency:
The Martin Agency
Creative Director:
Mike Hughes,
Jamie Mahoney
Art Director:
Jamie Mahoney
Copywriter:
Raymond
McKinney
Photographers:
Steve Vaccariello
(this page, top),
Ed Nielsen
(this page, bottom),
John Goodman,
(opposite, top left)
Chris Shorten
(opposite, top right),
Rodney Smith
(opposite, bottom left),
Howard Schatz
(opposite, bottom right)
Studio Artist:
Julie Lamb
Print Producers:
Linda Locks,
Melissa Ralston
Client:
Finlandia Vodka

In a past life, I was Nostradamus. Nothing, I mean nothing, surprises me.

In a past life I was pure, glacial spring water.

In a past life I was a fir tree. One day somebody chopped me down and covered me with decorations. Next thing I knew, they threw me back outside. I remember thinking, "What was that all about?"

In a past life I was pure, glacial spring water.

In a past life, I was Mrs. O'Leary's cow. Sorry, Chicago.

In a past life I was pure, glacial spring water.

In a past life, I was a pigeon in Central Park.
I thought humans were my slaves since they fed me all the time.

In a past life I was pure, glacial spring water.

In a past life I was a Merchant.
I used to trap the wind in bags
and sell them to sailors.

In a past life I was pure, glacial spring water.

In a past life, I lived in Atlantis. And you thought the Titanic was a disaster.

In a past life I was pure, glacial spring water.

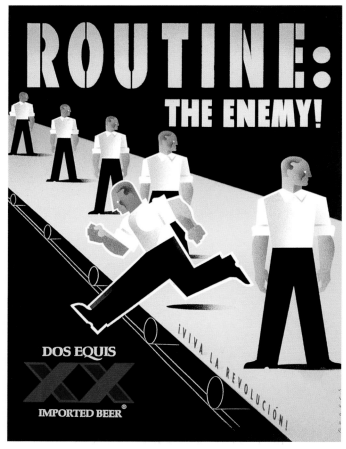

(opposite, top)
Agency: Ammirati Puras Lintas
Creative Directors:
Mark Johnson, Tom Nelson
Art Directors: Andrew Golomb
Copywriter: Larry Goldstein
Illustrator: Hard Times Coffee Cup
Client: Dos Equis

(opposite, bottom and this page)
Agency: Robaire and Hogshead/
The Martin Agency
Creative Directors:
Jean Robaire, Sally Hogshead
Art Director: Jean Robaire
Copywriter: Sally Hogshead
Photographer: Richard Daily
Print Producer: Angie Faunce
Client: Remy Amerique, Inc.

INHALE

Super-oxygenated water scientifically formulated to help you refresh, replenish and recover every time

(opposite)
Agency: Karacters
Design Group
Creative Director:
Maria Kennedy
Art Director:
Matthew Clark
Copywriter:
Ian Bray
Photographer:
Mark
Montizambert
Production Designer:
Todd Belcher
Producer:
Sue Wilkinson
Client: Clearly
Canadian
Beverage
Corporation

(this page, top)
Agency:
Fallon McElligott
Creative Director:
David Lubars
Art Directors,
Designers:
Rick Yamakoshi,
Sean Robertson
Copywriter:
Dave Pullar
Client: Miller Lite

(this page, bottom)
Agency:
Fallon McElligott
Creative Director:
David Lubars
Art Director:
Dean Hanson
Copywriter:
Joan Shealy
Client: Miller Lite

(this page)
Agency: Ammirati Puras Lintas
Creative Directors:
Mark Johnson, Tom Nelson
Art Director: Beth Kosuk
Copywriter: Brian English
Client: Bacardi

(opposite)
Agency: Mojopartners
Creative Director: Gaby Bush
Art Director: Denis Mamo
Copywriter: Adam Lance
Photographer: Erwin Olaf
Client: Remy Australie

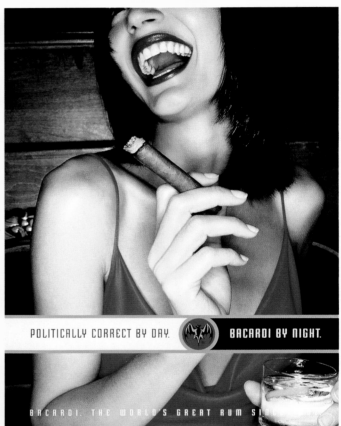

(opposite, top)
Agency:
The Richards Group
Creative Director:
Doug Rucker
Art Director: Kyle Friedel
Copywriter:
Cynthia Duxbury
Client: Chick-fil-A

(opposite, bottom)
Agency:
The Richards Group
Creative Director:
Doug Rucker
Art Director, Copywriter:
Dean Zostak
Client: Chick-fil-A

(this page)
Agency: Hoffman York
Creative Director,
Copywriter: Tom Jordan
Art Director, Designer:
Ken Butts
Tree: Atomic Props
Photographer: Scott Lanza
Client: Fiskars

IT'S LIKE PLAYING SPIN THE BOTTLE WITH A '61 BORDEAUX.

The technology of a serious camera. The spontaneity of a point-and-shoot. Now you don't have to choose between the two. The Nikon Pronea™ S is the best of both worlds. Serious camera technology. Compact size. Three picture formats. Interchangeable zoom lenses. At 16 ounces, it's one of the biggest things to happen to picture taking.

WE TAKE THE WORLD'S GREATEST PICTURES.™ YOURS.

See the affordable Pronea S and Nikkor lenses at authorized dealers displaying this symbol. ©1998 Nikon Inc. www.nikonusa.com or call 1-800-NIKON-35

LISTEN.

YOU CAN ALMOST HEAR THE PHOTO EDITOR PURR.

Nikon
WE TAKE THE WORLD'S
GREATEST PICTURES. YOURS.

The Nikon F5 System is designed to reduce the distance between the image in a photographer's mind and the
transparency on an editor's lightbox. For example, using an F5, a 300mm Nikkor lens and a Nikon speedlight,
Frans Lanting was able to illuminate this lion while preserving the subtle palette of the surrounding twilight. The final
image, not to mention his editor's reaction, is precisely what Frans had in mind. To learn more, call 1-800-NIKON-F5.

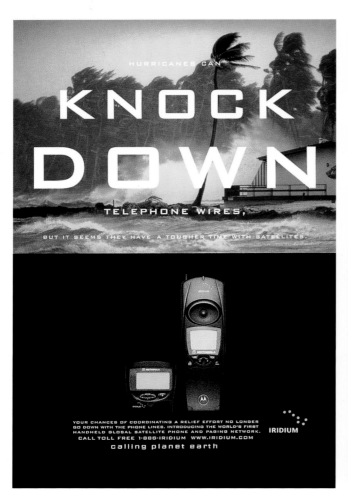
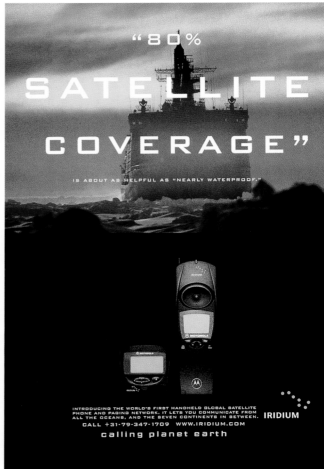
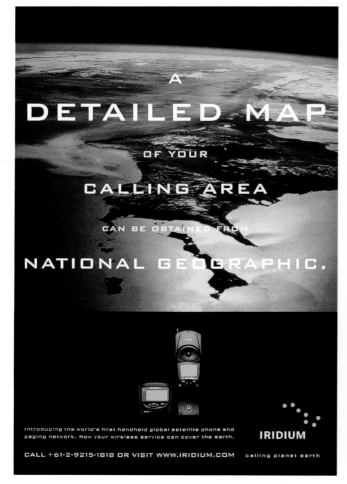
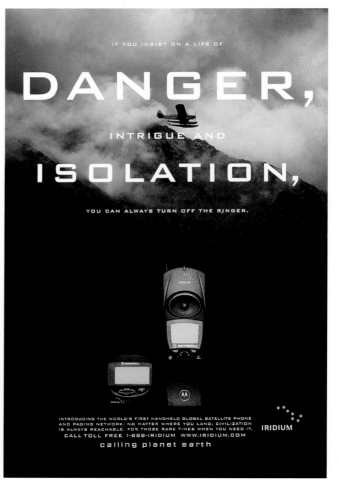

Agency: Ammirati Puris Lintas
Creative Directors:
Roger Bentley, Rob Feakins
Art Director: Gian Franco Arena
Copywriters:
Rob Feakins *(top left)*,
Michael Petsko *(bottom left)*,
Peter Kain *(right)*. Client: Iridium

(this page)
Agency: The Martin Agency
Creative Director,
Copywriter: Steve Bassett
Art Director: Jason Taylor
Illustrator: Brian

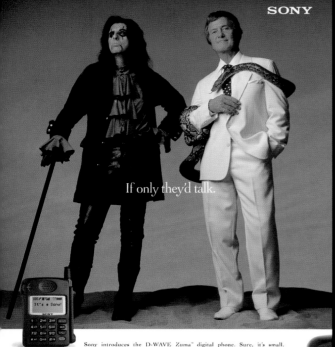

SONY

SONY

If only they'd talk.

If only they'd talk.

Sony introduces the D-WAVE Zuma™ digital phone. Sure, it's small. But it's powerful enough to bring people together who are worlds apart. (Even if they sing to a different drummer.) Our unique Jog Dial™ navigator finds your number so quickly, it's like the number finds you. And our microphone arm reaches down to catch your softest whispers. It's advanced technology that advances your life. So say what's on your mind. You can even sing it. The world will be a more harmonious place. Now you're talking.™

Jog Dial™ navigator. Just scroll, click and talk.

For information on Sony wireless products call 1-800-578-SONY or visit us at www.sony.com/wireless

Sony introduces the remarkable D-WAVE™ line of wireless phones. Like our D-WAVE Zuma™ digital phone. Sure, it's small. But it's powerful enough to bring people together who are worlds apart. (Even if they live in the same house.) Our unique Jog Dial™ navigator finds your number so quickly, it's like the number finds you. And our microphone arm reaches down to catch even your softest whispers. It's advanced technology that advances your life. So have a heart to heart. It'll make a world of difference. Now you're talking.™

For information on Sony wireless products call 1-800-578-SONY or visit us at www.sony.com/wireless

Agency:
Sawyer Riley Compton
Creative Director:
Bart Cleveland
Art Directors:
Tammy Thorn Anderson,
Bart Cleveland
Copywriters:
John Spalding, Brett Compton
Photographer: Joe Lampi
Client: Mitsubishi
Wireless Digital Cellular
Phones

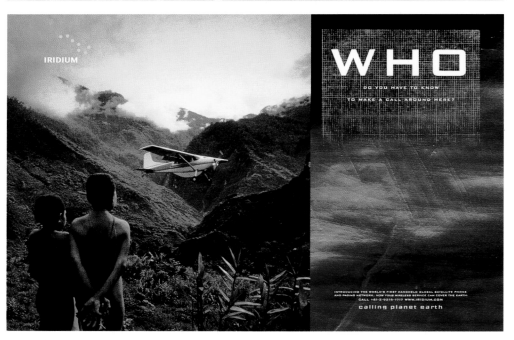

gigahit

digital

For James Cameron's "Titanic," DIGITAL AlphaServer™ systems ran nonstop for weeks, rendering thousands of frames of complex visual effects—beautifully and blazingly fast. If your business could use that kind of speed, power and reliability, there's only one way to go. With us. Find us at www.digital.com/gigahit or call 1-800-DIGITAL. And get ready to win in a networked world.

mesh

digital

In a world too ready to abandon the last great thing for the next great thing, we make all your IT investments—past, present and future—work as one well-oiled machine. We were voted #1 systems integrator, so whether it's OpenVMS,™ UNIX™ or Windows NT, no one's better at making it all work together. Find us at www.digital.com/mesh, or call 1-800-DIGITAL. And get ready to win in a networked world.

(this page)
Agency: Borders, Perrin
& Norrander
Creative Director: Terry Schneider
Art Director: Joel Nendel
Copywriter: Miguel Caballero
Photographer: Mark Ebsen
Client: La Cie

(opposite)
Agency: Saatchi & Saatchi
Creative Directors:
Steve Silver, Curtis Melville
Art Director: Curtis Melville
Copywriter: Steve Silver
Photographer: Dan Escobar
Client: Hewlett Packard

unix = foresight

unix = hp

Your data center holds the records of past and present events. It can also hold the key to future business opportunities, but only if you're able to quickly process and evaluate your

information. HP's UNIX solutions have the speed and strength you need to make critical business decisions. And to let you see what's ahead. For more info: www.hp.com/go/unix.

HEWLETT PACKARD

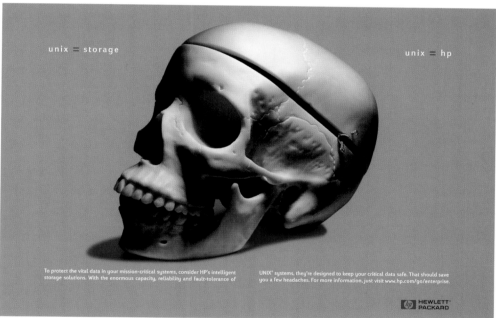

unix = storage

unix = hp

To protect the vital data in your mission-critical systems, consider HP's intelligent storage solutions. With the enormous capacity, reliability and fault-tolerance of

UNIX® systems, they're designed to keep your critical data safe. That should save you a few headaches. For more information, just visit www.hp.com/go/enterprise.

HEWLETT PACKARD

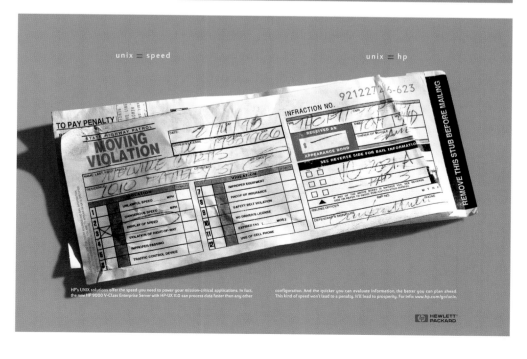

unix = speed

unix = hp

HP's UNIX solutions offer the speed you need to power your mission-critical applications. In fact, the new HP 9000 V-Class Enterprise Server with HP-UX 11.0 can process data faster than any other

configuration. And the quicker you can evaluate information, the better you can plan ahead. This kind of speed won't lead to a penalty. It'll lead to prosperity. For info: www.hp.com/go/unix.

HEWLETT PACKARD

Now you can print photo-quality images, on any paper. The HP DeskJet 722C uses special printing technology called PhotoREt II. Sharp detail and natural colors make for surprisingly lifelike realism. No matter what paper you use. Just $349. Visit www.hp.com/go/DJ722spider or a store near you. And see what extraordinary things you can do with ordinary paper.

Agency:
Goodby,
Silverstein
& Partners
Creative
Director:
Steve
Simpson
Art Director:
Jon Soto
Copywriter:
Al Kelly
Photographer:
Chris Callis
Client:
Hewlett
Packard

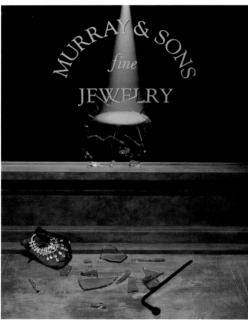

MURRAY & SONS
fine
JEWELRY

Now your business can print photo-quality images, on any paper. The HP DeskJet 890C uses special printing technology called PhotoREt II. Sharp detail and natural colors make for surprisingly lifelike realism, no matter what paper you use. All this, at up to 9 pages per minute, for just $449. Visit www.hp.com/go/DJ890jewel or a store near you. And see what extraordinary things you can do with ordinary paper.

Now your business can print photo-quality images, on any paper. The HP DeskJet 890C uses special printing technology called PhotoREt II. Sharp detail and natural colors make for surprisingly lifelike realism, no matter what paper you use. All this, at up to 9 pages per minute, for just $449. Visit www.hp.com/go/DJ890salesman or an Office Depot near you. And see what extraordinary things you can do with ordinary paper.

Now you can print photo-quality images, on any paper. The HP DeskJet 722C uses special printing technology called PhotoREt II. Sharp detail and natural colors make for surprisingly lifelike realism. No matter what paper you use. Just $349. Visit www.hp.com/go/DJ722wallpaper or a store near you. And see what extraordinary things you can do with ordinary paper.

Now you can print photo-quality images, on any paper. The HP DeskJet 722C uses special printing technology called PhotoREt II. Sharp detail and natural colors make for surprisingly lifelike realism. No matter what paper you use. Just $349. Visit www.hp.com/go/DJ722mouse or a store near you. And see what extraordinary things you can do with ordinary paper.

Now you can print photo-quality images, on any paper. The HP DeskJet 722C uses special printing technology called PhotoREt II. Sharp detail and natural colors make for surprisingly lifelike realism. No matter what paper you use. Just $349. Visit www.hp.com/go/DJ722locker or a store near you. And see what extraordinary things you can do with ordinary paper.

Agency: Communiqué Group
Creative Director:
Brian Dolinski
Art Director: James Wilkes
Copywriter: Brian Flay
Illustrator: Greg Banning
Typography: Bryan Banman
Client: Microsoft

Lee Garfinkel, Gary Goldsmith
Art Director: Chris Brignola
Copywriter: Jay Sharfstein
Photographer: David Robbins
Client: Sony Electronics

(this page)
Agency: Allen & Gerritsen
Creative Director,
Copywriter: Mick O'Brien
Art Director: Marcy Levey
Client: Sybase, Inc.

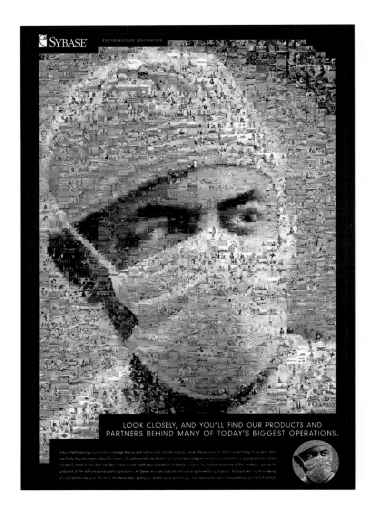

(opposite)
Agency: Ingalls
Creative Directors: Rob Rich,
Steve Bautista
Art Director: Rich Wallace
Copywriter: Martin Davidson
Photographer: Scott Keith
Client: Raytheon

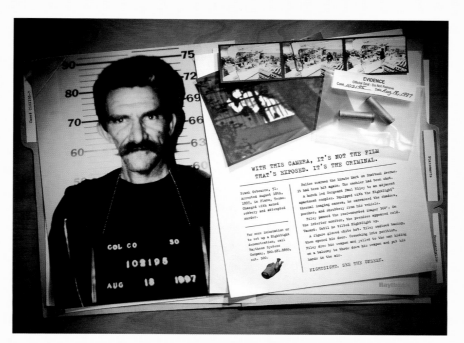

WITH THIS CAMERA, IT'S NOT THE FILM THAT'S EXPOSED. IT'S THE CRIMINAL.

NIGHTSIGHT. SEE THE UNSEEN.

FOR 13 YEARS, HE WAS ON THE RUN.
THEN, FINALLY, TECHNOLOGY CAUGHT UP WITH HIM.

NIGHTSIGHT. SEE THE UNSEEN.

CAUGHT IN ITS LENS, CRIMINALS EXPERIENCE SUDDEN APPREHENSION FOLLOWED BY ISOLATION AND GUILT.

NIGHTSIGHT. SEE THE UNSEEN.

WE CAN HELP YOU BUILD A BETTER _____.

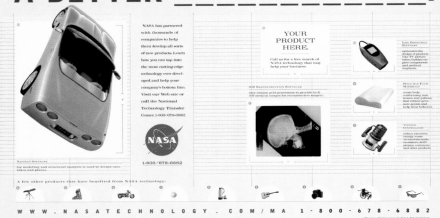

NASA has partnered with thousands of companies to help them develop all sorts of new products. Learn how you can tap into the most cutting-edge technology ever developed and help your company's bottom line. Visit our Web site or call the National Technology Transfer Center. 1-800-678-6882.

NASA
1-800/678-6882

YOUR PRODUCT HERE.

Call us for a free search of NASA technology that may help your business.

A few other products that have benefited from NASA technology:

BIG BRAINS FOR RENT.

Need help developing a new product? NASA brings you the most cutting-edge technology ever developed. Our engineers have partnered with thousands of companies to create all kinds of gizmos. Learn how we can help your company's bottom line. Visit our Web site or call us at the National Technology Transfer Center. 1-800-678-6882.

NASA
1-800/678-6882

YOUR PRODUCT HERE.

Call us for a free search of NASA technology that may help your business.

A few other products that have benefited from NASA technology:

GREETINGS EARTHLINGS.
WE BRING YOU GIFTS.

We bring you the most cutting-edge technology ever developed. Already, NASA has partnered with thousands of companies to help them develop new products. Learn how we can help your company's bottom line. Visit our Web site or call the National Technology Transfer Center. 1-800-678-6882.

NASA
1-800/678-6882

YOUR PRODUCT HERE.

Call us for a free search of NASA technology that may help your business.

A few other products that have benefited from NASA technology:

(opposite)
Agency: The Martin Agency
Creative Director: Hal Tench
Art Director: Noel Ritter
Copywriter: Raymond McKinney
Photographer: Kip Dawkins
Studio Artist: Tyson Brown
Print Producer: Marge Hickman
Client: NASA

The F-22 air dominance fighter: Equipped to destroy the enemy in the sky and on the ground on the first day of a war. Equally adept at destroying an enemy's desire to fight, long before there is a war.

www.f22-raptor.com

What does it take to prevent a war? The same strength it takes to win one. The revolutionary F-22 will give America uncompromised air dominance. And it will give potential adversaries a single option: Peace.

www.f22-raptor.com

(this page)
Agency: DDB Needham New York
Chief Creative Officers:
Steven Landsberg, David Nathanson
Executive Creative Director,
Copywriter: Giff Crosby
Art Director: David Nathanson
Photographer: Eric Schulzinger
Client: Lockheed Martin

(this page)
Agency: Ammirati Puris Lintas
Creative Directors:
Mark Johnson, Tom Nelson
Art Director: Scott Kaplan
Copywriter: Jason Holzman
Client: UPS

(opposite, left)
Agency: Ammirati Puris Lintas
Creative Directors:
Adam Goldstein, David Harner
Art Director: Lona Walburn
Copywriter: Mark Cacciatore
Client: UPS

(opposite, right)
Agency: BBDO Canada
Creative Directors: Michael
McLaughlin, Jack Neary
Art Director: Scott Dube
Copywriter: Ian MacKellar
Photographer: Philip Rostron
Client: FedEx Canada

Season's greetings from 330,000 of Santa's little helpers.

FedEx. Proud shipper of portfolios to the 1998 Strategy Magazine Agency of the Year Competition.

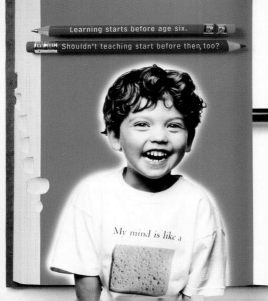

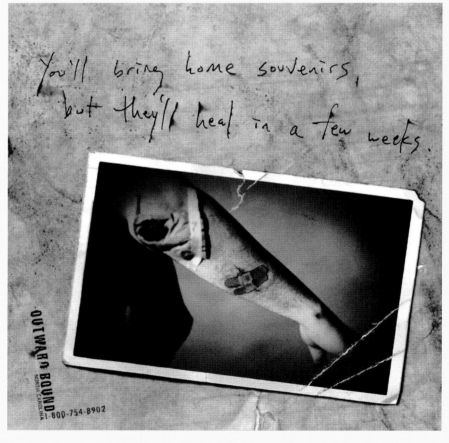

Agency:
Loeffler Ketchum Mountjoy
Creative Director: Jim Mountjoy
Art Director: Doug Pedersen
Copywriters:
Curtis Smith, Mike Duckworth
Photographer: Jim Arndt
Client: Outward Bound

COMMITTED TO AN ENVIRONMENT
WHERE STUDENTS DON'T HESITATE
TO ASK ONE ANOTHER FOR HELP.

It takes a special place to learn to do great advertising. A place where people know the way you get better is to help others. That's what we do, because that's who we are. Of course, by attending a school for art directors, copywriters, designers, illustrators and photographers, your need for help goes without saying.

THE CREATIVE CIRCUS
1-800-728-1590

Teaching the next generation of art directors, copywriters, designers, illustrators and photographers to be advertising revolutionaries requires a unique approach. However, we see no reason to abandon the age-old traditions of academia that made this the greatest country on earth.

The Creative Circus
1·800·728·1590

BUSINESS, MATH,

HISTORY, ARTS, SCIENCES,

JUDGMENT DAY.

YUP, EVERYTHING'S COVERED.

UNIVERSITY OF
ST.THOMAS
MINNESOTA

JUST IN CASE THE

MEEK

HAPPEN TO GET

SHORTED

ON THEIR INHERITANCE.

UNIVERSITY OF
ST.THOMAS
MINNESOTA

(this page)
Agency: Hammerquist
& Halverson
Creative Director:
Fred Hammerquist
Art Directors: Matt
Peterson, Mike Proctor
Copywriters:
Ian Cohen, Matt
McCain
Photographer:
Bob Peterson
Digital Artist:
Charlie Rakatansky
Client: Bicycle Alliance
of Washington

(opposite)
Agency: DGWB
Advertising
Creative Director:
Jon Gothold
Art Directors: Steve
Ricker, Joe Cladis
Copywriter:
Chris Cruttenden
Photographer:
Kevin Reimers
Client: Weinerschnitzel

CHARIOTS OF FIRE

Gates open at 4:00pm

Agency: Ruiz Nicoli
Creative Director: Ana Hidalgo
Art Director: Alvaro R. Solano
Copywriter: Carlos Jimeno
Photographer: Alfonso Zubiaga
Client: Guggenheim Bilbao
Museum

TWENTY-X JEANS FOR WOMEN.
By Wrangler.

Agency:
Neiman Marcus Advertising
Creative Director:
Georgia Christensen
Designer: Bennet & Elia
Photographer:
Giovanni Gastel
Client: Neiman Marcus

THIERRY MUGLER

NeimanMarcus

TSE NEW YORK

NeimanMarcus

MISSONI

NeimanMarcus

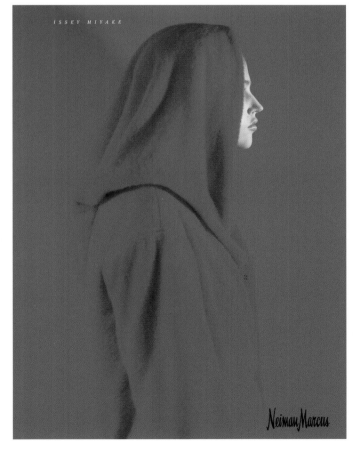

ISSEY MIYAKE

NeimanMarcus

COACH

CASSANDRA WILSON JAZZ SINGER

COACH

JULIE KENT DANCER, AMERICAN BALLET THEATRE

COACH

FOR THE HOLIDAYS

INTRODUCING THE NEW SLIM DUFFLE SAC

(opposite)
Agency: Toth Brand Imaging
Creative Director: Reed Krakoff
Art Director: Joanne Reeves
Photographers: Richard Burbridge,
Peter Lindberg. Client: Coach

(this page)
Agency: Austin Kelley Advertising
Creative Directors:
Mark Robinson, Jim Spruell
Art Director: Damon Williams
Copywriter: Duncan Stone
Illustrator: John Bills
Photo (right): Kansas State
Historical Society. Client: Barn Fly

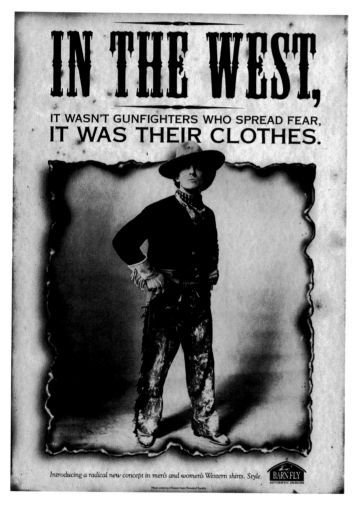

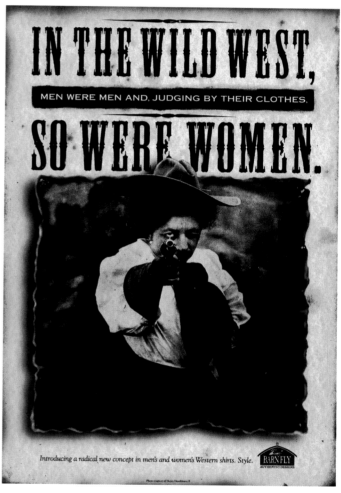

(this page)
Agency: The Martin Agency
Creative Director: Brian
Fandetti
Art Director: John Boone
Copywriter: David Oakley
Photographer: Gilles
Mingasson
Studio Artist: Matt Wieringo
Print Producer: Angela
Faunce
Client: Wrangler Company

(opposite)
Agency: TBWA/Chiat/Day
Creative Directors:
Lee Clow, Peter Angelos,
Rob Smiley
Art Director: Roz Romney
Photographer:
Michael McLaughlin
Client: Levi Strauss & Co.

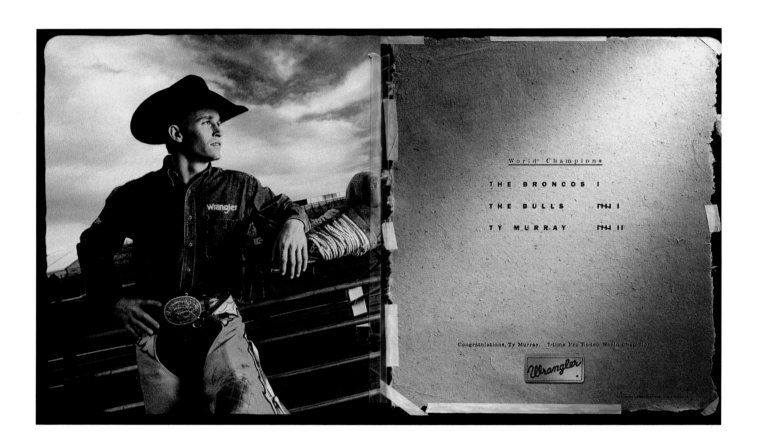

WHY BUDDY LEE'S INSURANCE AGENT HASN'T CANCELED HIS POLICY.

DESIGNED TO SURVIVE PLACES YOU WEREN'T.

These jeans were made to take a real beating. We use Lazy-Z bar-tacking at points of strain. The seams are double-stitched with heavyweight golden wheat thread. The waistband is lock-stitched to the jeans. In short, these pants can take just about anything time, nature, or fate can manage to dish out. Will them to someone you like.

M.O.A. NO. 7

BUDDY LEE IS ON ACTION LIKE STRIPES ON A SHIRT WITH A LOT OF STRIPES ON IT.

Behind the scenes with the man behind the man

"EXCLAMATION POINTS, THAT'S WHAT MAKES A GOOD BUDDY LEE SCRIPT."

Marty Friedman, "Man of Action" writer

Nothing says "action" like a script full of exclamation points. We recently sat down with "M.O.A." writer Marty Friedman, who offered a rare glimpse into the magic that is "Buddy Lee, Man of Action." Marty: "Buddy's a giver. That's what I would say. Always wanting to give the audience more. Most spokesbots I've worked with can only handle one, maybe two exclamation points in a script. Buddy demands no less than fifteen per page. The man is a giver."

OCCUPATIONAL RISK CHART

	LOW	HIGH
BEING BUDDY LEE		✗
CONVENIENCE STORE CLERK	✗	
MOB INFORMANT	✗	
FIREMAN	✗	
GARDENER	✗	

WARNING
EXPLOSIVES ARE HIGHLY EXPLOSIVE.
BUDDY LEE IS A TRAINED PROFESSIONAL.

WHEN BUDDY'S IN THE DRIVER'S SEAT, ACTION RIDES SHOTGUN.

www.leedungarees.com

Remember: always wear your seat belt.
Rugged jeans are no substitute for common sense.

Genuine · *Authentic* · Durable
Lee
DUNGAREES
CAN'T BUST 'EM
Since 1889

Guaranteed Quality Hardworking

Another reason we're able to say,
"NO DOLLS WERE INJURED IN THE MAKING OF OUR COMMERCIALS."

BUDDY LEE-TESTED.
I.E., STRONG ENOUGH FOR A DOLL, YET MADE FOR A HUMAN.

Each pair of Lee Dungarees is carefully stitched with heavyweight golden wheat thread. The back pockets are reinforced with Lazy-Z bar tacking. The waistband is lock-stitched to the jeans. And of course, only the most durable denim is used throughout. In other words, not only will these Lee Dungarees pass the tests of time, wear, and peril, they'll come back and beg for extra credit.

M.O.A. NO. 4

IF BUDDY HAD A MIDDLE NAME IT WOULD BE "ACTION." ALTHOUGH "CARL" IS NICE TOO.

BUDDY LEE, ACTION IS HIS BUSINESS, AND BUSINESS IS GOOD!

★ ★ ★ ½ ★

Critics agree.
"Buddy Lee, Man of Action is some of Buddy's best work."

WE USED 14-OUNCE, RING-SPUN DENIM BECAUSE CHAIN MAIL TENDS TO RUST.

In designing our new line of rugged denim jeans, we considered using many materials. These, being denim jeans, we finally decided on denim. But not just any denim—ring-spun denim—the most durable denim in the marketplace. Not only do the ring yarns add strength and a classic vintage look, they also have relatively little trouble with airport metal detectors.

REVERSE ANGLE

MISSOURI
FREIGHT & CARGO

THIS IS A MAP OF MISSOURI.

They say Buddy Lee has a backbone the size of Missouri. We're pretty sure they mean the actual state though. Which is even bigger than the map.

THINGS THAT ARE TOUGH.

calculus   diamonds   our jeans

$$y'[x] = 0.2y(x)$$
$$\text{with } y[0] = 1$$

10,000 FEET NO PARACHUTE, LOTS OF GRAVITY.

Warning: Buddy Lee is a trained professional. Remember, when jumping out of a plane, always use a parachute.

IT'S NOT THE FALL THAT HURTS, IT'S THE LANDING.

Genuine · *Authentic* · Durable
Lee
DUNGAREES
CAN'T BUST 'EM
Since 1889

Guaranteed Quality Hardworking

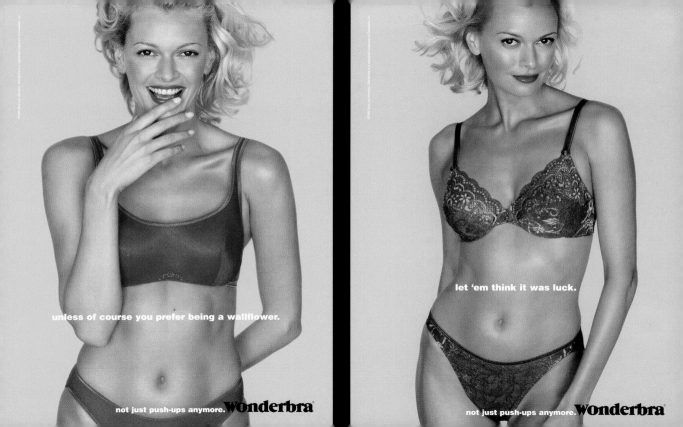

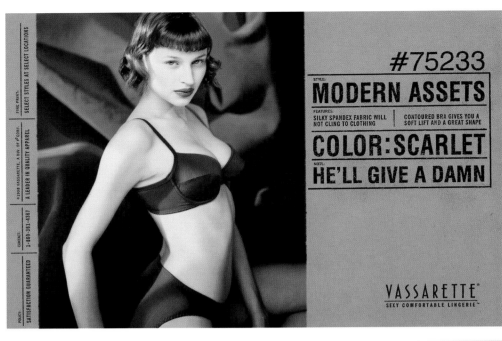

#75233

STYLE:
MODERN ASSETS

FEATURES:
| SILKY SPANDEX FABRIC WILL NOT CLING TO CLOTHING | CONTOURED BRA GIVES YOU A SOFT LIFT AND A GREAT SHAPE |

COLOR:SCARLET

NOTE:
HE'LL GIVE A DAMN

VASSARETTE
SEXY COMFORTABLE LINGERIE

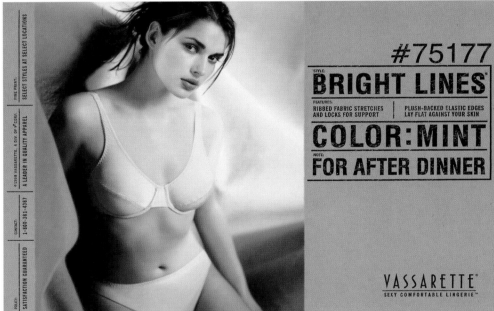

#75177

STYLE:
BRIGHT LINES

FEATURES:
| RIBBED FABRIC STRETCHES AND LOCKS FOR SUPPORT | PLUSH-BACKED ELASTIC EDGES LAY FLAT AGAINST YOUR SKIN |

COLOR:MINT

NOTE:
FOR AFTER DINNER

VASSARETTE
SEXY COMFORTABLE LINGERIE

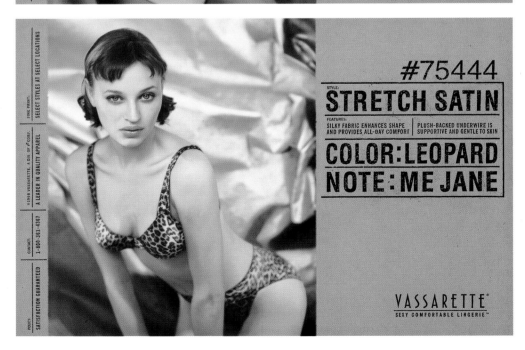

#75444

STYLE:
STRETCH SATIN

FEATURES:
| SILKY FABRIC ENHANCES SHAPE AND PROVIDES ALL-DAY COMFORT | PLUSH-BACKED UNDERWIRE IS SUPPORTIVE AND GENTLE TO SKIN |

COLOR:LEOPARD
NOTE:ME JANE

VASSARETTE
SEXY COMFORTABLE LINGERIE

(this page)
Agency:
The Martin
Agency
Creative
Director:
Mike Hughes
Art Director:
Mark
Wenneker
Copywriter:
Jeff Ross
Photographer:
Toni
Meneguzzo
Studio Artist:
Mark Brye
Print Producer:
Renee Carrano
Client:
Vassarette,
A Division
of Vf
Corporation

(opposite, top)
Agency:
Borders,
Perrin &
Norrander
Creative
Director:
Terry
Schneider
Art Director:
Kent Suter
Copywriter:
John
Heinsma
Photographers:
Sam Walsh,
R. J. Muna,
Dave Emmite
Client:
Columbia
Sportswear

(opposite, bottom)
Agency:
Borders,
Perrin &
Norrander
Creative
Director:
Terry
Schneider
Art Director:
Tia Doar
Copywriter:
Troy Asplund
Photographers:
R. J. Muna,
Dave Emmite
Client:
Columbia
Sportswear

A BASE CAMP WITH ARMS AND A HOOD.

Chairman Gert Boyle

Why lug around 20 sherpas and a tent when all the protection you need is right on your back? Strap on an Icefield Parka™ and you'll be ready for just about anything. Waterproof, breathable Omni-Tech CXB™ fabric with durable Mini-Faille Omni-Tech™ reinforcements prepares you for the worst. A wicking mesh lining and radial vents keep you from steaming up inside. A zip-out MTR Fleece™ liner insulates against unexpected blizzards. And an integral pullout storm hood is always there when you need it. Returning to base camp has never been easier. For the dealer nearest you call 1-800-MA-BOYLE. www.columbia.com

◆ **Columbia**
Sportswear Company.

FRIGID PERHAPS.

COLD NEVER.

Throughout her life, Chairman Gert Boyle has been called many things. Cold, however, has never been one of them. Probably something to do with the Boulder Ridge Parka™ that she is never without. She designed it herself using the Columbia Interchange System,™ with a Bergundtal Cloth™ shell and Bergundtal Ripstop II™ reinforcements on the outside, zip-out Perfecta Cloth™ and MTR Fleece™ lining on the inside. Because if there's one thing she's learned in 74 years, it's how to stay warm. For the dealer nearest you call 1-800-MA-BOYLE. www.columbia.com

◆ **Columbia**
Sportswear Company.

(this page, top)
Agency: Borders, Perrin &
Norrander
Creative Director: Terry Schneider
Art Director: Tia Doar
Photographer:
Raphael Astorga
Client: Columbia Sportswear

(this page, bottom)
Agency: Borders, Perrin &
Norrander
Creative Director: Terry Schneider
Art Director: Tia Doar
Copywriter: Troy Asplund
Photographer: Mark Hooper
Client: Columbia Sportswear

(opposite)
Agency: McGarrah/Jessee
Creative Directors:
Doug Irving, Bryan Jessee
Art Director: Judy Engelman
Copywriter: Matt McCaffree
Photographer: John Katz
Type Designer: Don Grimes
Client: Mike Mitchell,
Savane/Farah

SAVANE 8-WALE CORDUROY PANTS.
VERY SOFT. VERY COMFORTABLE.

SAVANE

PURVEYORS OF STYLE
WWW.SAVANE.COM

SAVANE COMFORT STRETCH™ PANTS.
100% COTTON. 100% COMFORTABLE.

SAVANE

PURVEYORS OF STYLE
WWW.SAVANE.COM

SAVANE COMFORT STRETCH™ PANTS.
100% COTTON. 100% COMFORTABLE.

SAVANE

PURVEYORS OF STYLE
WWW.SAVANE.COM

If kids could pick the colors

Dreamakers. Sleepwear by Carter's. Colors by kids. *Carter's*
"If they could just stay little 'til their Carter's wear out."

If kids could pick the colors

Dreamakers. Sleepwear by Carter's. Colors by kids. *Carter's*
"If they could just stay little 'til their Carter's wear out."

WORKOUT GEAR BY CRUNCH

WORKOUT GEAR BY CRUNCH

(this page)
Agency: Saatchi & Saatchi
Creative Directors: Steve Silver,
Curtis Melville
Art Director: Joe Kayser
Copywriter: Rob Jamieson
Photographer: Bob Mizono
Client: E-LOAN

(opposite)
Agency: Grace & Rothschild
Creative Director: Ray Grace
Designer: Patrick Sutherland
Copywriter: Kristen Livolsi
Photographer: Steve Bronstein
Print Director: Abby Demillo
Client: Ernst & Young

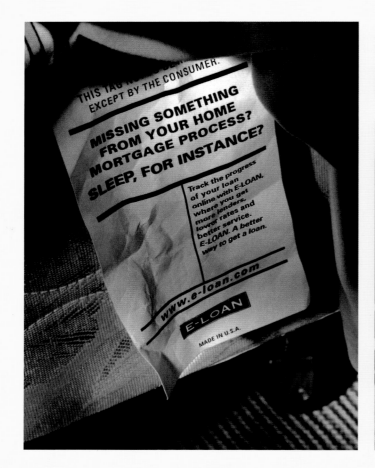

Fire

LIFT

Police

LIFT

Ernst & Young

LIFT

THERE ISN'T A BUSINESS WE CAN'T IMPROVE™ ⊟| ERNST & YOUNG

©1998 ERNST & YOUNG LLP

www.ey.com

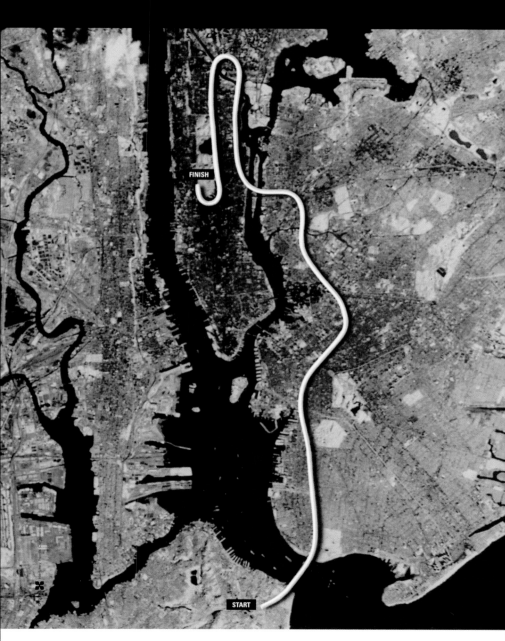

Agency: DDB
Needham New York
Chief Creative Officers:
David Nathanson,
Steven Landsberg
Art Director: Andy Dijak
Copywriter: David Lowe
Photographer: Larry Sillen,
FPG International
Client: Hershey Foods
Corporation, Ronzoni

FINISH

START

OFFICIAL PASTA OF THE 1998 NEW YORK CITY MARATHON®

RONZONI   SPAGHETTI·8
PASTA

(this page)
Agency: Heye + Partner, Vienna
Creative Director,
Copywriter: Alexander Bartel
Designer: Frank Widmann
Photographer: Niko Schmidt Burgk
Client: McDonald's Austria

(opposite)
Agency: The Richards Group
Creative Director: Glenn Dady
Art Director: Shane Altman
Copywriter: Stuart Hill
Illustrator: Steve Pietzch
Photographer: Tom Ryan
Production Manager: Todd Gutman
Computer Artist: Betsy Perkins
Client: The Catfish Institute

Verdi's operas, Shakespeare's comedies, Trudy's baked Catfish.

TRUDY'S BAKED
PECAN-DIJON CATFISH

Bravo.

Paper or plastic? Boxers or briefs? Grilled or fried?

GRILLED CATFISH   FRIED CATFISH

Whatever.

Man on the moon, Women on the Supreme Court, Catfish on the grill.

GRILLED CATFISH
WITH CITRUS MARINADE

Here's to forward thinking.

Painless dentistry, wrinkle-free cotton, baked Catfish.

BAKED CATFISH
PARMESAN

Progress is neat, huh?

(this page)
Agency: Publicis & Hal Riney
Executive Creative Directors:
John Doyle, Dave O'Hare
Art Director: John Emmert
Copywriter: Mark Sweeney
Illustrator: David Hughes
Client: Clif Bar

(opposite)
Agency: BBDO Canada
Creative Director:
Michael McLaughlin
Art Director: Wally Krysciak
Copywriter: Rob Tait
Photographer: Garth Grosjean
Client: Kraft Canada

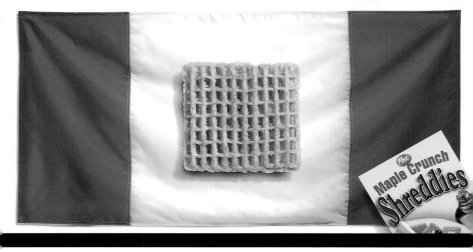

CHESTNUT   Pine   **Maple**

Birch   **OAK**   Maple

(this page)
Agency: Butler Shine & Stern
Creative Directors:
John Butler, Mike Shine
Art Director: Hilary Wolfe
Illustrator: Harry Bliss
Copywriter: Ryan Ebner
Client: Jamba Juice

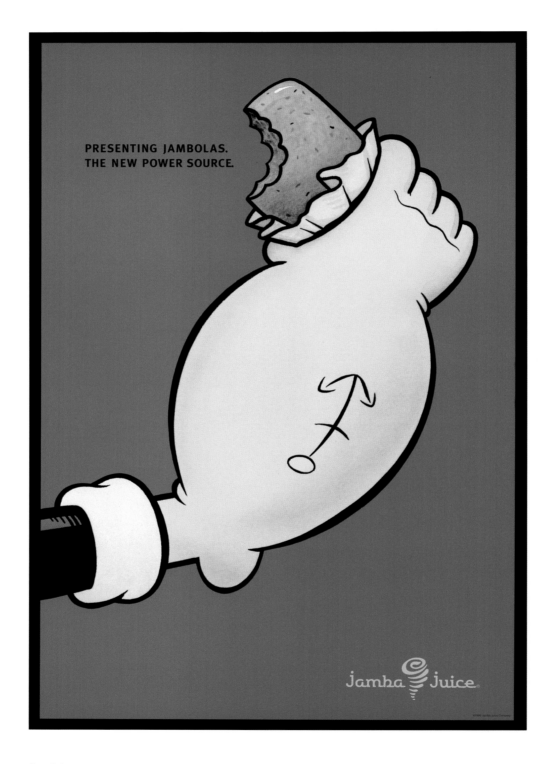

(opposite)
Agency: Allen & Gerritsen
Creative Directors: Mick O'Brien,
Doug Chapman
Art Director: Marcy Levey
Designer: Tracy Schroder
Copywriter: Mike Davis
Photographer: Richard Schultz
Client: Exeter Health Resources, Inc.

Panel 1 (top left)

IN HEALTH CARE, WHAT WALKS

LIKE A DUCK

AND TALKS LIKE A DUCK

MAY NOT, IN FACT, BE

A DUCK.

[body text]

YALE NEW HAVEN HEALTH
A Story with a Happy Beginning

Panel 2 (top right)

THERE MAY NEVER BE

A CURE

FOR RISING HEALTH CARE COSTS.

BUT, AT LEAST, THERE'S AN

ANTIDOTE.

[body text]

YALE NEW HAVEN HEALTH
A Story with a Happy Beginning

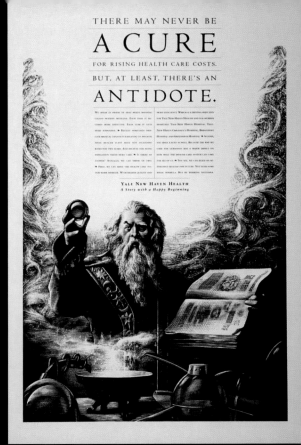

Panel 3 (bottom left)

TO TAKE ON MODERN HEALTH CARE,

YOU NEED TO BE CLEAR OF

VISION,

PURE OF HEART,

and just a little hard of head.

[body text]

YALE NEW HAVEN HEALTH
A Story with a Happy Beginning

Panel 4 (bottom right)

WHEN IT COMES TO

CANCER,

THE IMPOSSIBLE

DREAM

IS NO LONGER IMPOSSIBLE.

[body text]

YALE NEW HAVEN HEALTH
A Story with a Happy Beginning

(opposite)
Agency: Sandstrom Design
Art Director, Designer:
George Vogt
Copywriter: Jef Loeb
Illustrator: Mark Summers
Client: Yale New Haven Hospital

(this page)
Agency: Foley Sackett
Creative Director: Ron Sackett
Art Director: Tim Moran
Copywriter: Johnny Mackin
Photographer: Mark LaFavor
Client: Blue Cross and Blue
Shield of Minnesota

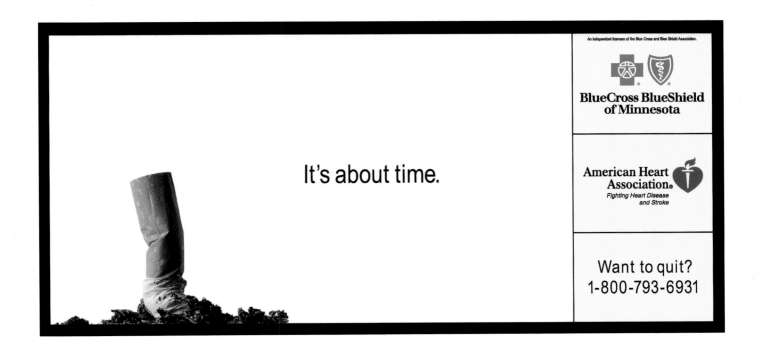

Elitär? Vielleicht. Es gibt über 400 Versicherungsgesellschaften. Eine hat in ihrem Programm die Markenversicherung NAUTIMA. Bei der Entwicklung dieses exklusiven Konzepts haben wir an alles gedacht, um Boots- und Yachteignern optimalen Schutz zu bieten. Zum Beispiel auch an ein spezielles Helpline-Handy. Festprogrammierte Tasten sorgen jederzeit für schnelle Hilfe bei technischen oder medizinischen Notlagen. Ganz gleich, ob vor Sylt oder vor Mallorca. Wir beraten Sie gern persönlich über die neue Sicherheit an Bord.

Mannheimer

Was sammeln Sie? Porzellan aus Meißen? Uhren aus Glashütte? Bronzen aus Wien? Was immer Ihre Passion ist, Sie kämen wohl nie auf die Idee, Ihre Sammlung als simplen Hausrat einzustufen. Normale Versicherungen tun das aber. Die Folge: Ihre Werte sind nur eingeschränkt versichert. Mit ARTIMA bieten wir Ihnen eine Allgefahrenversicherung, die auch Transportschäden, Diebstahl und sogar persönliches Mißgeschick einschließt. Sagen Sie uns, was Sie sammeln, und wir machen Ihnen ein persönliches Angebot.

Mannheimer

Das Risiko, alt zu werden. Nie war die Lebenserwartung so hoch wie heute. Aber auch nie waren die Aussichten so ungewiß. Kann man seinen Lebensstandard halten? Oder droht der Sozialfall? Welche Pflege erhält man, wenn man bedürftig wird? Fragen, auf die wir gute Antworten haben. Zum Beispiel unsere Markenversicherung HUMANIS. Sie beginnt dort, wo die gesetzliche Pflegeversicherung aufhört zu zahlen. Wie der Name schon sagt, sichert sie nicht nur Lebensstandard und Pflege, sondern auch Ihre Würde.

Mannheimer

Wichtige Karriere-Regel: Delegiere komplexe Bereiche. In jeder Generation gibt es Menschen, die mehr von sich und dem Leben erwarten. Für diese Menschen haben wir die neue Markenversicherung PRIMOS entwickelt. PRIMOS ist ein Rundum-Versicherungskonzept, das alle wichtigen Risiken checkt und umfassend löst. Gemacht für Singles und Doppelverdiener, die festen Boden unter ihre Karriere bringen wollen, sich aber nicht unnötig lange mit dem Thema Versicherungen beschäftigen möchten.

Mannheimer

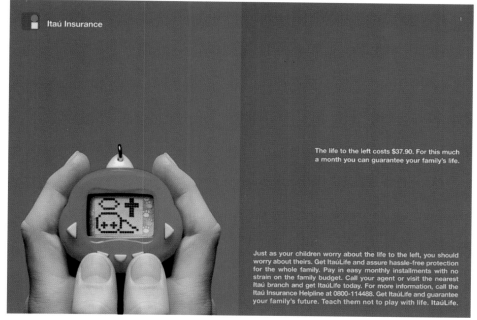

(opposite)
Agency:
Beithan Hessler
Werbeagentur
GmbH
Art Director:
Peter Hessler
Designer:
Susanne Schaefer
Copywriter:
Jochen
Beithan
Photographers:
Bernd Nörig,
Carsten Görling
Client:
Mannheimer
AG Holding

(this page)
Agency:
DM9DDB
Publicidade
Creative
Directors:
Tomás Lorente,
Nizan Guanaes
Art Director:
Tomás Lorente
Copywriter:
Carlos
Domingos
Photographer:
Alexandre
Catan
Client:
Itau Insurance

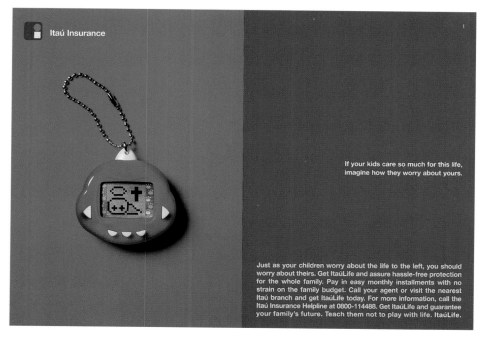

(this page)
Agency: The Romann Group
Creative Director:
Gad Romann
Art Director, Designer:
Marta Ibarrondo
Designer: Erez Bahar
Copywriter: Aimee Heller
Photographer: Carl Flatow
Client: Auction Universe

(opposite)
Agency: Slaughter Hanson
Advertising
Creative Directors:
Gary Brandon, Terry Slaughter
Art Director,
Copywriter: Gary Brandon
Designers:
Gary Brandon, Liz Rybka
Client: Safe Quest

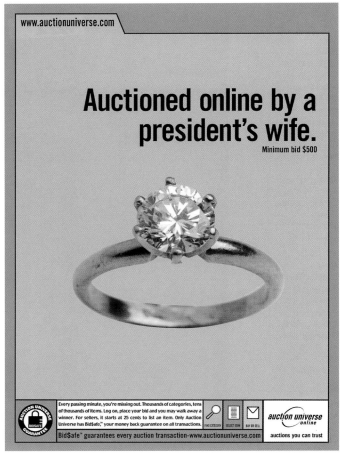

Would you do your homework if you could watch Miss January take a shower instead?

Maybe you can't be there every time your kids log on to the Internet, but we can. With SafeQuest, you not only get great Internet service, you can block 99.9% of all pornography, violence and hate-oriented Web sites before they even enter your home. So why risk anything less? Get SafeQuest for just $19.95 per month. To order, contact us at 1-800-SafeQuest or www.safequest.com.

SAFEQUEST
The Web without the worry.

See no evil.

Sure, there's some scary stuff on the Internet, but that doesn't mean you have to look at it. With SafeQuest, you not only get great Internet service, you can block 99.9% of all pornography, violence and hate-oriented Web sites before they even enter your home. So why risk anything less? Get SafeQuest for just $19.95 per month. To order, contact us at 1-800-SafeQuest or www.safequest.com.

SAFEQUEST
The Web without the worry.

Frustrate a pedophile today.

At last, an Internet Service Provider that separates the men from the boys – literally. With SafeQuest, you not only get great Internet service, you can block 99.9% of all pornography, violence and hate-oriented Web sites before they even enter your home. So why risk anything less? Get SafeQuest for just $19.95 per month. To order, contact us at 1-800-SafeQuest or www.safequest.com.

SAFEQUEST
The Web without the worry.

NEDY FACES AN ENEMY MORE
AN COMMUNISM: RACISM.

"MR. PRESIDENT, MARTIN LUTHER KING ON LINE 1,
GEORGE WALLACE ON LINE 2."

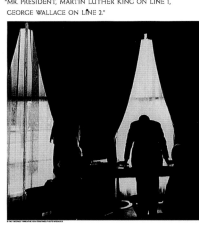

Relive the civil rights
movement of the 60s.
The John F. Kennedy
Library & Museum
617-929-4523

(opposite)
Agency: The Martin Agency
Creative Director: Hal Tench
Art Director: Cliff Sorah
Copywriter: Joe Alexander
Photographer: Charles Moore *(left)*,
George Tames, N.Y. Times
Photo Archive *(right)*
Studio Artist: Ailse Long
Print Producer: Linda Locks
Client: John F. Kennedy
Library Foundation

(this page)
Agency: Butler Shine & Stern
Creative Directors:
John Butler, Mike Shine
Art Director, Designer:
Bradley Wood
Copywriter: Dean Wei
Client: Chicago Jazz Museum

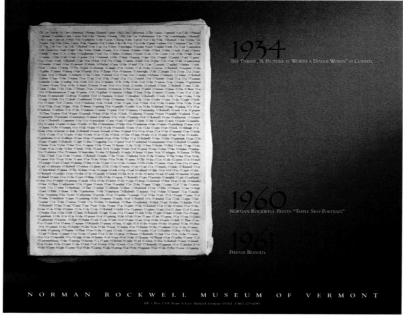

(this page)
Agency: Allen & Gerritsen
Creative Directors:
Mick O'Brien,
Doug Chapman
Art Director: Marcy Levey
Copywriter: Jim Elliott
Photographer:
Jack Richmond
Client: The Norman Rockwell
Museum

(opposite)
Agency: Publicis & Hal Riney
Creative Director:
John Doyle
Art Director: Kelly Dekin
Copywriter: Sean Austin
Client: Nantucket Whaling
Museum

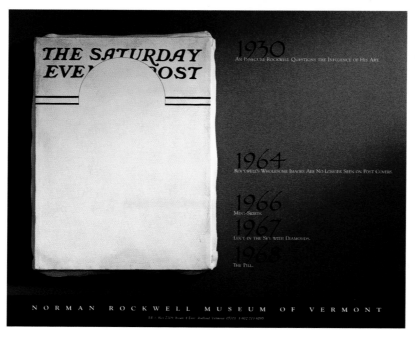

THE SPERM WHALE'S DIET CONSISTS MOSTLY OF SQUID. BUT YOU KNOW HOW HARD IT IS TO STAY ON A DIET.

Right whales were fairly easy to catch, because they were sluggish and not very aggressive. And when attacked, they simply dove—almost as if you'd sunk them. But the sperm whale was a different matter. They fought back. And when they did, it was a bench clearer.

The sperm whale would use its tail to slash and slap at the whaling boat. And with a single blow, they could easily crush both the boat and the people inside it.

Whalers who had seen this tail, or heard about it, called it the Hand of God. (And we're pretty sure they meant the wrathful, Old Testament version.)

Sperm whales would also do something known as "jawing back," in which they roll from side to side, snapping and chewing at anything within reach. The trick of course, was to stay out of their reach. But apparently, this was not always an easy thing to do.

THEY HAVE THE LARGEST BRAINS IN THE WORLD. AND STILL PEOPLE ONLY WANT THEM FOR THEIR BODIES.

What people wanted, of course, was oil, which came from blubber. And no whale contained as much blubber, or as much oil as the bowhead. Their tongue alone could contain as much as 25 barrels. And their lips could contain 60.

The sperm whale, on the other hand, had something even more valuable than oil: a thick, milky substance called spermaceti, which was contained in their enormous heads. And this is where it starts to get a little weird.

To collect the spermaceti, two or possibly three naked men would climb into the cavity of the head. Wade up to their hips in the snow-white fat. And use buckets to ladle it out.

For many people, this raises two questions: Who was the first person to think of doing this? And why naked? To which we can only reply: Don't know. And why not.

And let us not forget ambergris. Ambergris is a substance that forms around undigested squid beaks, in the intestines of a sperm whale. And when mixed with perfumes and incense, it heightens and prolongs their scents. It was also used as an aphrodisiac. Of course, it was never shown to have any effects as an aphrodisiac. But you have to remember that humans have relatively small brains. And sometimes it takes them a while to catch on.

Director: Hal Barber
ywriter: Susan Willoughby
ctor of Print Production:
y Hoerler
nt: Neenah Paper

PRESENT BRILLIANT CREATIVE TO CLIENT

REVISION ONE

PRESENT TO CLIENT

REVISION TWO

PRESENT TO CLIENT

REVISION THREE

PRESENT TO CLIENT

REVISION FOUR

APPROVED BY CLIENT

IT'S STILL BRILLIANT

MAKE SURE YOUR PAPER IS WORTHY

NEENAH PAPER

ONE ALL-NIGHTER

DAYS OF RETOUCHING JUST FOR THE COMP

UNUSED CONCERT TICKETS

NETWORK GOES DOWN. AGAIN

FIRST SIGN OF CARPAL TUNNEL SYNDROME

BEST OPPORTUNITY OF THE YEAR

MAKE SURE YOUR PAPER IS WORTHY

Brights, Whites, Duplexing, Envelopes, Laser and Ink Jet Guarantee, Announcements, Labels, Duplexes, Double Thick Covers

ONE ALL-NIGHTER

DAYS OF RETOUCHING JUST FOR THE COMP

UNUSED CONCERT TICKETS

NETWORK GOES DOWN. AGAIN

FIRST SIGN OF CARPAL TUNNEL SYNDROME

BEST OPPORTUNITY OF THE YEAR

MAKE SURE YOUR PAPER IS WORTHY

New co

Double thick covers

Duplexes

Laser and inkjet compatible

NEENAH PAPER

Matching envelopes

(this page, left)
Agency: Youngcom!
Design Firm: Das Labor
Art Director: Markus Weissenhorn
Copywriter: Michael Simperl
Photographer: Sascha Kletzsch
Client: Cibavision Switzerland

(this page, right)
Agency: Youngcom!
Design Firm: Das Labor
Art Director: Markus Weissenhorn
Copywriter: Michael Simperl
Photographer: Ralf Kiefner
Client: Cibavision Switzerland

(opposite)
Agency: ACI
Art Director: Simon Kuo
Client: Viagra

WOW

Ask your doctor to find out more about Viagra.

EGO

Ask your doctor to find out more about Viagra.

HOPE

Ask your doctor to find out more about Viagra.

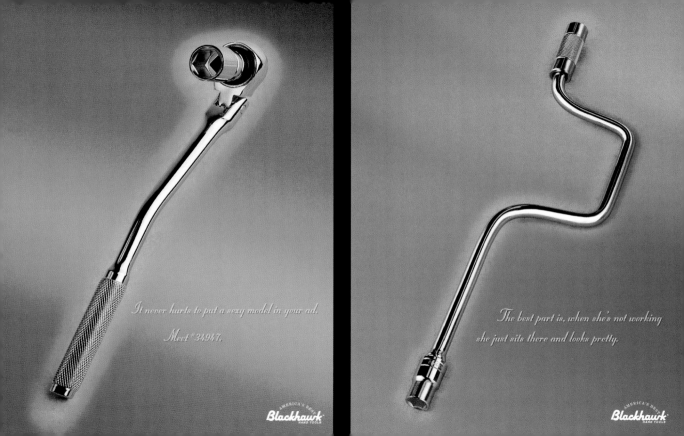

It never hurts to put a sexy model in your ad.

Meet #34947.

The best part is, when she's not working
she just sits there and looks pretty.

Blackhawk HAND TOOLS · AMERICA'S BEST

Blackhawk HAND TOOLS · AMERICA'S BEST

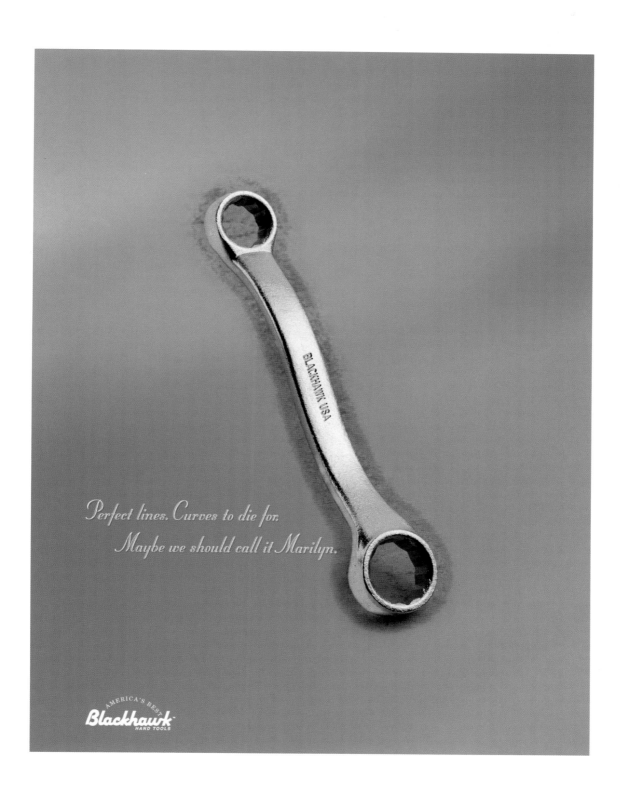

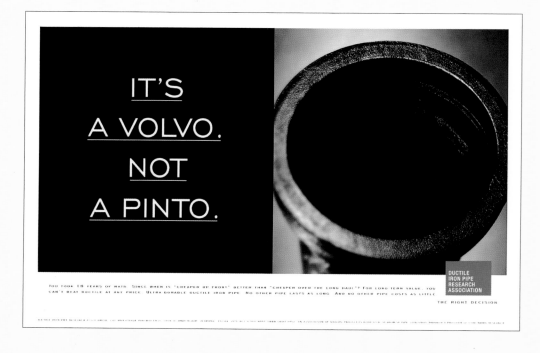

For the finest in hand-tied, river-tested fly cuisine, choose Idylwilde flies.

Stop by booth #624 at the Fly Fishing Retailer World Expo, and sample Idylwilde's extensive

collection of nymphs, streamers, saltwater and dry flies. Idylwilde Flies. Will work as food.™

An Idylwilde fly is not your normal fly. Hand-crafted to

exacting standards, customers as well as fish eat them up as fast as they can.

To learn more about reasonably priced Idylwilde flies, please give us a call.

Idylwilde Flies   820 N. River Street   Suite 205   Portland, OR 97227   503-288-2990

Idylwilde Flies   820 N. River Street   Suite 205   Portland, OR 97227   503-288-2990

(this page)
Agency: Ruiz Nicoli
Creative Directors: Ana Hidalgo,
Eduardo Contreras, Arturo Lopez
Art Director: Eduardo Contreras
Photographer: Rosa Muñoz
Copywriter: Arturo Lopez Rodriguez
Client: Tornado

T@RNADO
MAXIMUM STRENGHT

/ 57

(opposite)
Agency: Slaughter Hanson
Advertising
Creative Director, Copywriter:
Terry Slaughter
Art Director: Paul Crawford
Photographer: Geoff Knight
Client: Momentum Textiles

"Before my father sold insurance, he was a jazz musician. Saxophone. 1968. New York. He lived in a high-rise apartment building. A small group of fellow jazz players always played together at the end of the day up on the roof. Hot summer sunsets looking down on the rooftops. My father gave up his jazz career but not his jazz. Every evening growing up he gave me a saxophone serenade. Miles Davis, Wayne Shorter, Roger Ayers. All the Greats. But his favorite was Miles Davis. This was my fondest memory of my father. On a recent trip, feeling rather beat down, I rode trancelike the glass elevator to my high-rise hotel room. And then I heard it. Over the elevator sound system. Miles Davis. It was the end of the day and the rooftops below me glowed in the setting sun." *Momentum Designer*

MOMENTUM
TEXTILES

"Well, one afternoon I saw this dog and he was walking down an alley. I think maybe it was August. Maybe it was July. Anyway, it was hot. I remember it was hot because I saw those kind of invisible heat waves coming off the pavement. And this dog stops, looks back at me. It was as if he was asking me for a drink of water. But then he turns and walks away. As he steps into the street, one of those big package delivery trucks comes to a screeching halt. The dog frantically jumps back onto the sidewalk. A grocery clerk is stacking red apples in front of the grocery store and as the dog jumps back, the dog collides with the grocery clerk and scatters red apples all onto the pavement. The dog runs away." *Momentum Designer*

MOMENTUM
TEXTILES

"A holly bush grew outside the bedroom window of my childhood home. It was my protector. I felt it kept monsters and bad guys from breaking in because every point on every leaf was capable of inflicting pain. It was natural barbed wire. For 18 years I believed it kept me from harm. My family has since moved away but I recently visited my childhood home. I walked the grounds and quickly came to the external view of my bedroom. The holly bush was still there, but long neglected. It was almost bare. No longer the deterrent to evildoers, its leaves now blanketed the ground. And then I saw it. A small crack in the bedroom window. As if someone had recently tried to get in." *Momentum Designer*

MOMENTUM
TEXTILES

"One of those arrow signs blinked the message I was looking for—'The Blue Room. Hot Jazz 2nite. $2 cover!' It was on the wrong side of town. It had always been. Even in college. But it was a magical place. And part of the magic was the decor. Black lights made designs on the ceiling glow like the Milky Way. Names, messages and doodles scratched by students over the decades. It had been 20 years since I was last at the Blue Room. The smoke was just as thick, the jazz was just as hot, but the graffiti galaxy had grown. For hours I just listened to the jazz and gazed at the ceiling. And then I saw it. Glowing with the rest of the constellation. Three short words. 'Jazz is Oxygen.' Scratched below it was a date, 1971. And a name. A familiar name. Mine." *Momentum Designer*

MOMENTUM
TEXTILES

没 题

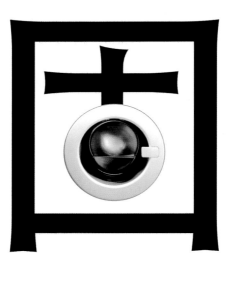

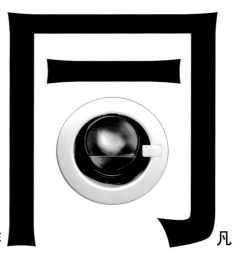

非 凡响

(opposite)
Agency: Lowe &
Partners/Monsoon
Creative Director: Khee Jin Ng
Art Director: Thomas Yang
Copywriters: Mandy Siow,
Vijayan Ganesh
Photographer:
Dong, Test Shot Studio
Typographer: Thomas Yang
Client: Sanyo
Malaysia Sdn Bhd

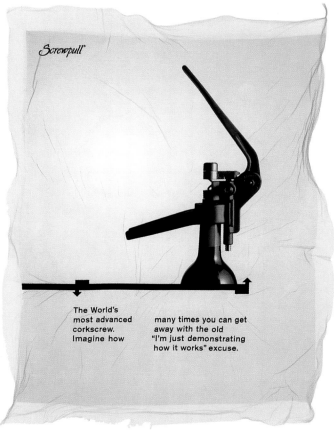

(this page)
Agency: TBWA/GGT
Simons Palmer
Creative Director: Trevor Beattie
Art Director: Paul Belford
Copywriter: Nigel Roberts
Photographer: Laurie Haskell
Client: Le Creuset

Agency: Loeffler
Ketchum Mountjoy
Creative Director,
Art Director:
Jim Mountjoy
Copywriter: Curtis Smith
Client: Velux

It was a dark and stormy night.

Cool.

skylights and roof windows
VELUX®

Some see dragons.

Some see islands.

What do you see?

skylights and roof windows
VELUX®

(this page)
Agency: FGI
Creative Director, Copywriter:
Denzil Strickland
Art Director: Rick Kourchenko
Photographer: GOZO
Client: PacFab

GLOBAL WARMING WILL CAUSE A SIGNIFICANT RISE
IN WATER TABLES. WE CAN HANDLE THAT.

You're into pools, we're into pools. From filtering to heating to lighting, you can trust
PacFab products. Call us reliable, call us committed. For that matter, call us obsessed.

THEY HAVE THEIR FIELD OF DREAMS,
WE HAVE OURS.

Not everyone thinks about pools 24 hours a day. We do. And we're just as obsessive
about standing behind our products. From heating to filtering to lighting, we never stop.

PacFab LET'S GO SWIMMING

PacFab LET'S GO SWIMMING

(opposite)
Agency: Butler Shine & Stern
Creative Directors:
John Butler, Mike Shine
Art Director: Patrick Plutchow
Copywriter: Ryan Ebner
Photographer: Heimo
Client: Specialized Bicycles, Inc.

Agency: Ingalls
Creative Directors: Rob Rich,
Steve Bautista
Art Director: Wade Devers
Copywriter: John Simpson
Photographer: Jack Richmond
Client: Exoticar

THE DIRT CONTROL TIRE. BECAUSE YOU ALREADY ATE ENOUGH DIRT IN KINDERGARTEN.

Presenting the new Dirt Control™ and Dirt Master™ tires. The speed you expect from a slick tire, without sacrificing the traction and predictability of a full knobby tire in any condition, their shallow knob design blows the dirt (so you don't) while their super-light weight lets you maintain speed. It's the perfect marriage. Superior speed meets predictable traction. Plus, Inter-Casing™ XC technology adds to the package by making the Dirt Control and Dirt Master tires both durable and pinch-flat resistant. And, if they don't outperform your other tires, we'll replace them for free. So try them. Because, mountain biking should not feel like Power Bars® Not trails.

THE UNMATCHED CORNERING, DURABILITY AND SPEED OF THE 1998 TURBO TIRE. IT'LL MAKE THE HAIR ON THE BACK OF YOUR NECK STAND UP. UNLESS YOU'VE ALREADY SHAVED THAT TOO.

www.specialized.com

MOUNTAINS SHOULD TAKE MILLIONS OF YEARS TO FORM. NOT CLIMB.

(opposite)
Agency: William Eisner/Associates
Creative Director:
Chuck Schiller
Art Director: Taylor Smith
Copywriter: G. Andrew Meyer
Photographer: Allan Knox
Client: Koch Industries

(this page)
Agency: Hoffman York
Creative Director: Tom Jordan
Art Director,
Designer: Ken Butts
Copywriter: Mark Catterson
Photographer: Scott Lanza
Client: Fiskars

(this page)
Agency: Concrete Design
Communications
Designer: Claire Dawson
Art Directors: Diti Katona,
John Pylypczak
Photographer: Ron Baxter Smith
Client: Umbra

(opposite)
Agency: Hoffman York
Creative Director, Copywriter:
Tom Jordan
Art Director, Designer: Ken Butts
Photographer: Dave Jordano
Client: Mautz

What misses one wall might find another.

What misses one wall might find another.

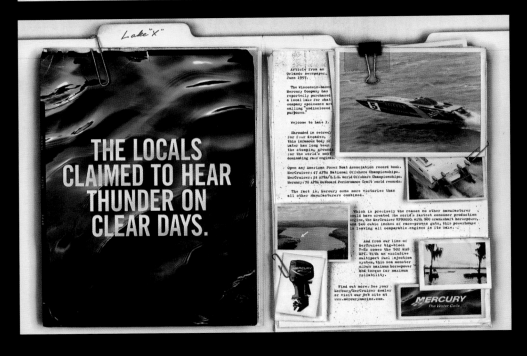

VICTOR
V.
MOUSE TRAPS

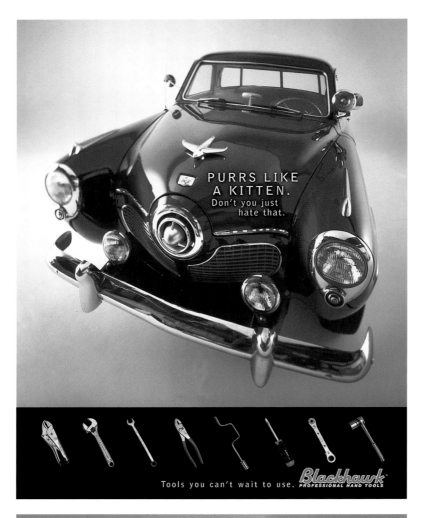

PURRS LIKE
A KITTEN.
Don't you just
hate that.

Tools you can't wait to use. *Blackhawk®*
PROFESSIONAL HAND TOOLS

MINT
CONDITION.
Bummer.

Tools you can't wait to use. *Blackhawk®*
PROFESSIONAL HAND TOOLS

(this page)
Agency: William Eisner / Associates
Creative Director: Chuck Schiller
Art Director: Taylor Smith

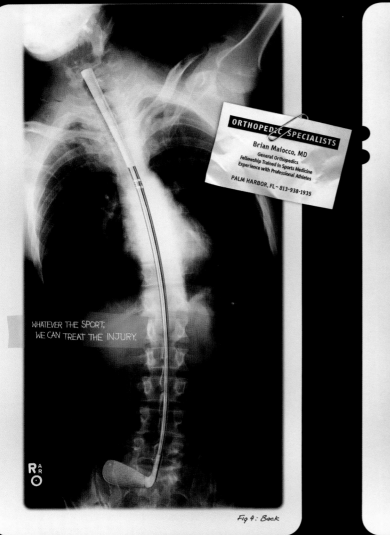

WHATEVER THE SPORT,
WE CAN TREAT THE INJURY.

ORTHOPEDIC SPECIALISTS

Brian Maiocco, MD

General Orthopedics
Fellowship Trained in Sports Medicine
Experience with Professional Athletes

PALM HARBOR, FL ~ 813-938-1935

Fig 4: Back

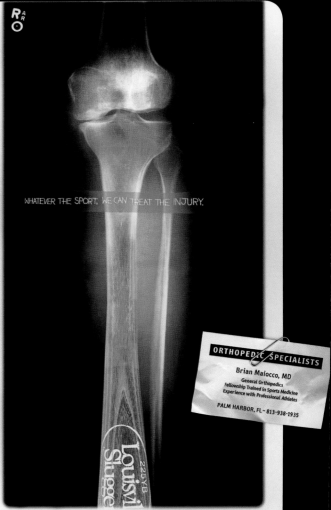

WHATEVER THE SPORT, WE CAN TREAT THE INJURY.

ORTHOPEDIC SPECIALISTS

Brian Maiocco, MD

General Orthopedics
Fellowship Trained in Sports Medicine
Experience with Professional Athletes

PALM HARBOR, FL ~ 813-938-1935

Fig 3: Knee joint

NO STOPPING

NO PARKING

NO WAITING FOR A FRIEND

NO JUST RUNNING IN FOR A SECOND

NO NOTHING

NO PARKING

TOW AWAY

UNLESS IT'S A MONDAY.
AND YOU'RE A GEMINI.
AND YOU DRIVE A 4-DOOR.
WITH WHITE WALLS.
AND IT'S A FULL MOON.
AND YOU SPEAK SWAHILI.
FLUENTLY. AND YOU...

(CONTINUED ON NEXT SIGN)

2 HOUR PARKING

↑

THE BIG PRINT GIVETH

AND THE FINE PRINT TAKETH AWAY

↓

FOR TOWED CARS PHONE 533-1235

Business Arenas

WASHINGTON, D.C. CHARLOTTE ATLANTA RESEARCH TRIANGLE PARK

WOMBLE
CARLYLE
OUR LAWYERS
MEAN BUSINESS

Stomping Grounds

ATLANTA   CHARLOTTE

WASHINGTON, D.C.   RESEARCH TRIANGLE PARK

WOMBLE
CARLYLE
OUR LAWYERS
MEAN BUSINESS

(opposite)
Agency: Greenfield/Belser
Creative Director: Burkey Belser
Designer: Jeanette Nuzum
Copywriters: George Kell,
Lise Anne Schwartz
Photographer: John Burwell,
Burwell & Burwell Studios
Client: Womble Carlyle

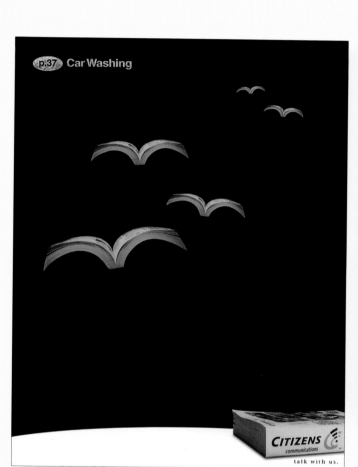

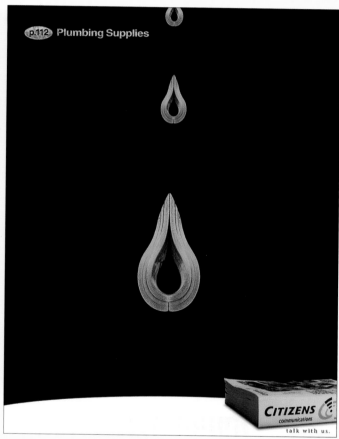

(this page)
Agency: Ingalls
Creative Directors: Rob Rich,
Steve Bautista
Art Director: Jim O'Brien
Copywriter: Martin Davidson
Photographer: John Holt
Client: Citizens Communications

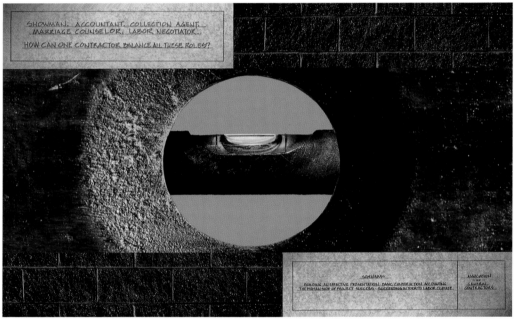

(opposite)
Agency: Loeffler Ketchum
Mountjoy
Creative Director, Art Director:
Jim Mountjoy
Copywriter: Ed Jones
Photographer: Jim Arndt
Client: Carolinas Associated
General Contractors

(this page)
Agency: McConnaughy Stein
Schmidt Brown
Creative Directors: Jim Schmidt,
Tom McConnaughy
Art Director: Jon Wyville
Copywriter: Kevin Lynch
Photographer: Darran Rees
Client: Illinova

Agency: TBWA Chiat/Day
Creative Directors:
Chuck Bennett, Clay Williams

Art Director: Jason Stinsmuehlen
Copywriter: Mark Abellera
Photographer: Craig Cutler Client: Kinko's.

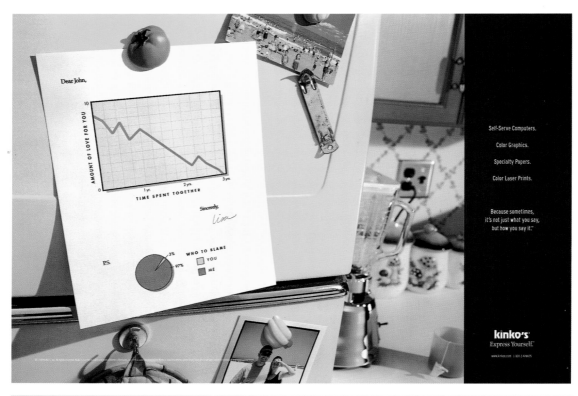

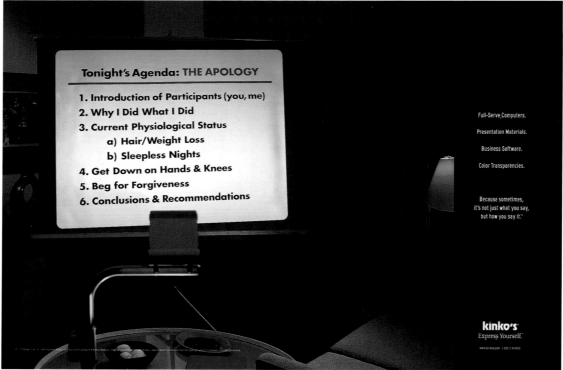

Agency: FGI
Creative Director, Copywriter:
Denzil Strickland
Art Director: Nick Law
Photographer:
Parish Kohanim
Client: Plastic Surgery Center

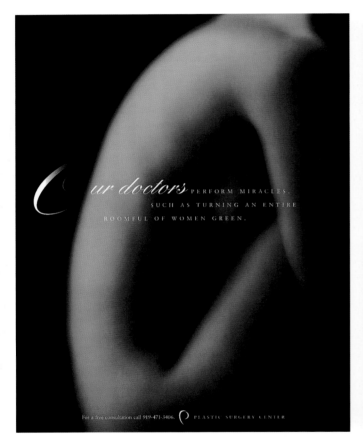

Our doctors PERFORM MIRACLES,
SUCH AS TURNING AN ENTIRE
ROOMFUL OF WOMEN GREEN.

For a free consultation call 919-471-3406. PLASTIC SURGERY CENTER

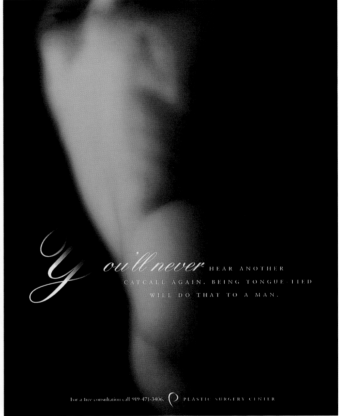

You'll never HEAR ANOTHER
CATCALL AGAIN. BEING TONGUE-TIED
WILL DO THAT TO A MAN.

For a free consultation call 919-471-3406. PLASTIC SURGERY CENTER

Agency: Greenberg Seronick
O'Leary and Partners
Creative Directors:
Gary Greenberg, Peter Seronick
Art Director: Kevin Daley
Copywriter: Craig Johnson
Photographer: Jack Richmond
Client: Portfolio

Concept Pad

concept pad

A fine, thin 11 lb. sulphite tracing paper for roughs and thumbnails. Approximately 77% transparency. Comes in pads or rolls.

Size	Item	List	
9"x12"	16-0022	$7.70	$5.79
11"x14"	16-0023	9.50	6.99
14"x17"	16-0024	15.40	11.49
19"x24"	16-0025	26.00	19.49

50 yd. rolls
12"	16-0026	$14.05	$11.29
18"	16-0027	20.75	17.69
24"	16-0028	23.60	19.99
30"	16-0029	35.75	29.99

Layout Pad

layout pad

Medium weight, 37 lb. tracing paper with a fine tooth surface and good body. Approximately 67% transparency. 75 sheets per pad. Also available in 50 lb.

Size	Item	List	
9"x12"	16-0030	$8.75	$6.99
11"x14"	16-0032	11.80	9.49
14"x17"	16-0034	17.75	14.29
19"x24"	16-0036	33.35	26.69
19"x24"	16-0037	35.35	28.69

Immediate shipping................

390 Graphics Pad

Heavyweight, 100% rag layout paper for any marker. Ink will hold a sharp edge without bleeding through. Pure white sheets with good translucency.

Size	Item	List	
9"x12"	16-1038	$7.35	$5.69
11"x14"	16-1039	9.95	7.99
14"x17"	16-1040	14.25	11.49
19"x24"	16-1041	27.50	21.99

Heavy Trace

heavy trace

Heavyweight, 50 lb. tracing paper for comps, illustrations and storyboards. Approximately 50% transparency, 80 sheets per pad.

Size	Item	List	
9"x12"	16-0042	$8.75	$6.99
11"x14"	16-0043	11.80	9.49
14"x17"	16-0044	17.75	14.29
19"x24"	16-0045	33.35	26.69

151 Design Pad

Natural vellum, layout and tracing paper featuring a smooth surface and superior transparency. Perfect for comps or finished art in pencil or pen. Good tearing strength and erasability. Resists cracking, 56 lb.; 50 sheets per pad. Also available in 100 sheets.

Size	Item	List	
9"x12"	16-0057	$13.25	$8.99
11"x14"	16-0058	17.50	12.99
14"x17"	16-0059	26.25	18.69
19"x24"	16-0060	51.50	38.59

50 yd. rolls
12"	16-0161	$14.05	$11.29
18"	16-0162	20.75	17.69
24"	16-0163	23.60	19.99
30"	16-0164	35.75	29.99
36"	16-0165	37.60	32.29

Art Director

Visual thinker, able to execute ideas with proficiency. Essential for print and broadcast advertising, direct marketing and collateral. A huge selection, from award-winning to workhorse. Sorry, no hacks in stock.

(See also copywriter, illustrator, graphic designer, Web site designer and desktop publisher.)

Attention freelancers: You too can be included in our catalog.

http://www.portfolio.skill.com

TO PLACE AN ORDER CALL
1-888-88-FOLIO.

Plain rolls
36"	16-0166	$14.05	$11.29
42"	16-0167	20.75	17.69

50 yd. rolls
12"	16-0168	$14.05	$11.29
18"	16-0169	20.75	17.69
24"	16-0170	23.60	19.99
30"	16-0171	35.75	29.99

Plain rolls
12"	16-0172	$14.05	$11.29
42"	16-0173	20.75	17.69
48"	16-0174	23.60	19.99

Ledger 950 Pad

ledger

Heavy 32 lb. sulphite paper is ideal for all dry media, pencil, pen and ink, felt marker and light paint. Perfect for drawing. 93% transparency. 50 sheets per pad.

Size	Item	List	
9"x12"	16-0150	$7.10	$5.99
11"x14"	16-0151	9.40	7.79
14"x17"	16-0152	12.75	10.79
19"x24"	16-0153	23.25	19.79

Bristol

Authentic 2-ply pasted sheets made to rigid specifications. The surface is hard yet receptive to any medium. Excellent erasability. Available in vellum (textured) or plate (smooth) surfaces. 20 sheets per pad.

Size	Item	List	
9"x12"	16-0100	$8.15	$5.99
11"x14"	16-0101	10.45	7.79
14"x17"	16-0102	15.50	11.59
19"x24"	16-0103	31.60	26.99
20"x30"	16-0104	33.50	31.99

Daley Graphics 360 Pad

Medium weight, 100% rag layout paper for felt markers. Ink will hold a sharp edge without bleeding through. Pure white sheets with good translucency.

Size	Item	List	
9"x12"	16-3367	$7.35	$5.69
11"x14"	16-3368	9.95	7.99
14"x17"	16-3369	14.25	11.49
19"x24"	16-3370	27.50	21.99

50 yd. rolls
12"	16-3371	$14.05	$11.29
18"	16-3372	20.75	17.69
24"	16-3373	23.60	19.99
30"	16-3374	35.75	29.99

Plain rolls
| 36" | 16-3375 | $37.60 | $32.29 |
| 42" | 16-3376 | 42.29 | 36.69 |

CALL FOR PRICING AND AVAILABILITY.

WRITING TOOLS

AMBASSADOR SERIES
Modern styling with consistent, skid-free writing.

A Roller Ball Pens

No.	Cap	Barrel	Each
RBP-840-1	Black Lacquer	Black Lacquer	$160
RBP-841-1	Chrome	Black Lacquer	$145

EMPIRE SERIES
Classic design, precise weight distribution for more comfortable writing.

B Roller Ball Pens
Roller ball performance with elegant styling.

No.	Description	Each
BPP-840-2	Chrome-Black Lacquer	$125
BPP-840-3	Chrome-Lapis	$125

C Ballpoint Pens
Unique clip design won't allow clipping to coat or shirt pocket with point out.

No.	Description	Each
BPP-2555-2	Palladium Plate	$16
BPP-2780-2	Chrome-Black Lacquer	$32

PORTFOLIO SERIES
Creative professionals available for temporary or permanent employment.

D Copywriter
Non-retractable head is full of ideas and can translate them into words. Can be used for print and broadcast advertising, direct marketing and collateral. A huge selection available. *(See also art director, illustrator, graphic designer, print production, photographer and desktop publisher.)*

Attention freelancers: You too can be included in our catalog.

portfolio

CALL PORTFOLIO AT 1-888-88-FOLIO.
http://www.portfolio.skill.com

E Roller Ball Pens
Superior ink flow and feel.

No.	Description	Each
BPP-2797-2	Black w/ Chrome Accent	$55
BPP-2443-2	Black Lacquer	$32

FINE LINE SERIES
Sleek easy-to-grip design features a pocket clip and a twist mechanism.

F Ballpoint Pens

No.	Description	Each
RBP-841-2	Chrome	$19

All the above pens carry the manufacturer's full lifetime warranty and come with a standard black ink refill.

(top, bottom)
Agency:
The Martin
Agency
Creative Director,
Copywriter:
Joe Alexander
Art Directors:
Kenny Sink,
Tyson Brown
Client:
Stretch Ledford
Photography

(middle)
Agency:
Bremner Design
Creative Director,
Art Director,
Photographer:
Craig Cutler
Designer:
Scott Bremner
Client:
NY Gold Book

(opposite)
Agency:
Bremner Design
Creative Director,
Art Director,
Photographer:
Craig Cutler
Designer:
Scott Bremner
Client: Select 47

Craig Cutler
212·473·2892

REPRESENTED
by Marzena
212·772·2522

Agency: Sandstrom Design
Creative Directors:
Steve Sandstrom, Steve Sandoz
Designer: Steve Sandstrom
Copywriter: Steve Sandoz
Photographers: Steve Bonini *(left)*,
Mark Hooper *(right)*
Client: Pavlov Production

XVI

PAVLOV **RESEARCHERS** SUCCESSFULLY **MATE** GNOMES WITH FROZEN **VEGETABLES**

EXHIBIT A: *Gnome*

EXHIBIT B: *Frozen Vegetables*

After years of experimentation (and the accidental creation of a few hideous sheep-like creatures), the researchers at PAVLOV PRODUCTIONS have perfected another tool designed to turn consumers into virtual buying machines. No, we're not talking about genetic engineering, we're talking about visual effects. The directors at PAVLOV PRODUCTIONS have the experience to make them look great, as opposed to some horrible industrial mishap. Which means you now have the ability to mate gnomes with frozen vegetables, shiny new cars, soft drinks or whatever else your twisted mind can envision. That should be enough to make anyone happy. Except, of course, the gnomes. PAVLOV PRODUCTIONS. 310-244-8941.

XXI

HOW TO MAKE AN **ORDINARY** SPOT PERFORM **MORE** LIKE A **PAVLOV** COMMERCIAL.

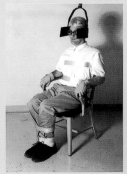

ITEM No.S46: VIEWING HARNESS (ADJUSTABLE)

ITEM No.S47: ELECTRO-STIMULATING CUSHION

In a perfect world, every commercial you create would be produced by PAVLOV PRODUCTIONS. But sometimes factors like the client's nephew who makes films prevent you from using PAVLOV and our patented behavioral modification techniques. That's why we've created these two simple devices to make ordinary commercials a little more riveting. The Viewing Harness, with optional Eye-Lid Restraints, holds the target's head firmly (yet not actually dangerously) in place. And the Electro-Stimulating Cushion* administers a variable shock to help focus viewer attention. Of course, these are poor substitutes for the overwhelming manipulative power of a genuine PAVLOV commercial, but at least they can help keep those lesser spots from being completely ignored. PAVLOV PRODUCTIONS, 310-244-8941.

*Requires separate 400 volt power supply.

(left)
Agency: Butler, Shine & Stern
Creative Directors:
John Butler, Mike Shine
Art Director: Hajime Ando
Copywriter: Dean Wei
Illustrator: Lucho Ortega
Client: Specialized Bicycles, Inc.

(right)
Agency: Socio X
Creative Director, Art Director:
Bridget de Socio
Designer: Jason Endres
Copywriter: Janou Pakter
Digital Imaging: Ninja Von Oertzen
Photographer: Andre Thijssen
Client: Janou Pakter Inc.

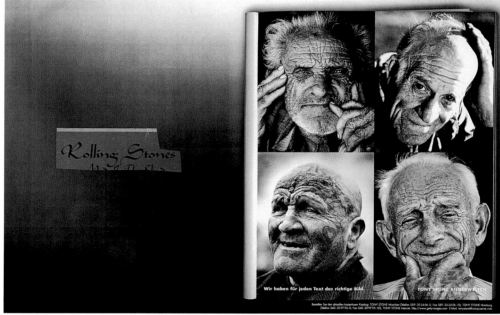

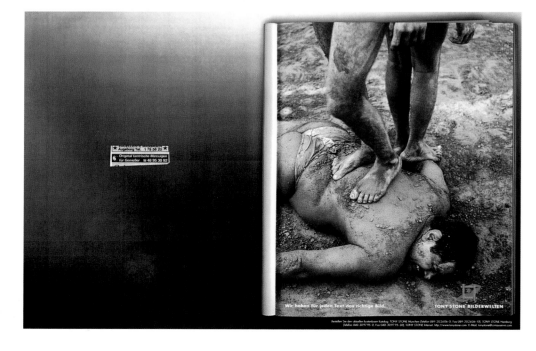

Luke Sullivan speaks on the art of simplifying your concepts.

At the next AD/CC meeting, Fallon's Luke Sullivan will be discussing simplicity in advertising. Coincidentally, he'll also be signing his new book, *Hey Whipple, Squeeze This*. April 16th at the Quest Garden Room, 110 N 5th Street. Food & drink at 5:30. Luke's opening shots at 6:30. Free for AD/CC members. Non-members, $30. Students, $15. RSVP by April 14th at 338-0177 or www.adccmpls.org. 3Com Palm Pilot drawing sponsored by Digital Minds. And just to complicate things, student awards will end the evening.

(this page)
Agency: McCann Erickson,
Geneva
Creative Director: Frank Bodin
Art Director: Urs Hartmann
Copywriter: Stefan Gigon
Photographer: Urs Maurer

(opposite)
Agency: Butler Shine & Stern
Creative Directors:
John Butler, Mike Shine
Art Director, Designer:
Bradley Wood
Copywriter: Ryan Ebner
Client: Canadian
Parapalegic Association

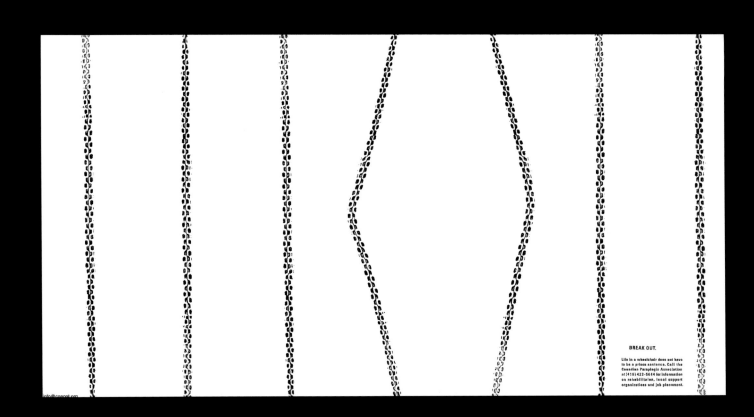

BREAK OUT.

Life in a wheelchair does not have
to be a prison sentence. Call the
Canadian Paraplegic Association
at (416) 422-5644 for information
on rehabilitation, local support
organizations and job placement.

info@cnipol.org

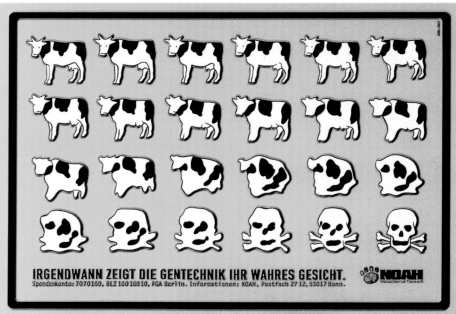

(opposite, top)
Agency: Jung Von Matt
Creative Directors: Hermann
Waterkamp, Frank Dovidar
Art Directors: Goetz
Ulmer, Lars Kruse
Designer: Corinna Falusi
Copywriter: Thomas Wildberger
Photographer: Nico Weymann
Client: Noah

(opposite, middle)
Agency: Jung Von Matt
Creative Directors: Hermann
Waterkamp, Frank Dovidar
Art Directors: Goetz
Ulmer, Lars Kruse
Designer: Corinna Falusi
Copywriter: Jan Kesting
Illustrator: Roland Warzecha
Client: Noah

(opposite, bottom)
Agency: Jung Von Matt
Creative Directors:
Hermann Waterkamp,
Frank Dovidar
Art Directors:
Goetz Ulmer, Lars Kruse
Designer: Corinna Falusi
Copywriter: Jan Kesting
Client: Noah

(this page)
Agency: Pollak Levitt + Nel
Creative Director: André Nel
Art Director, Designer:
Paul Huggett
Copywriter: Jeff Cole
Photographer: Tom Abraham
Client: Aid Atlanta

(this page)
Agency: Greenberg Seronick
O'Leary and Partners
Creative Directors:
Gary Greenberg, Peter Seronick
Art Director: Kevin Daley
Copywriter: Rick McHugh
Photographer: Al Fisher
Client: Mayor's Office/Office
of Consumer Affairs

(opposite)
Agency: Fahlgren/Tampa
Creative Director: Scott Sheinberg
Art Director: John Stapleton
Copywriter: James Rosene
Photographer: Tracy Brooks
Client: Mission: Wolf

WOLVES COMMUNICATE WITH EACH OTHER
BY HOWLING.

CONSIDERING WHAT WE'VE BEEN DOING TO THEM,
SCREAMING WOULD SEEM MORE APPROPRIATE.

They call out to each other in the darkness. But will those calls travel far enough to reach you? Once abundant in the wild,

the gray wolf has become scarce. But with your help, Mission: Wolf can continue their efforts to preserve this misunderstood animal.

You've heard their call. Please let us hear yours. Call (719) 746-2919 or write Mission: Wolf at P.O. Box 211, Silver Cliff, CO 81249.

 Mission: Wolf

COLD, WINTER WINDS
ARE NOT ENOUGH TO PENETRATE
THE WOLF'S THICK COAT.

IF ONLY THE SAME WERE TRUE OF BULLETS.

Nearly 200 years ago, more than half a million gray wolves roamed North America. Today, that number has plummeted to less

than 12,000. But with your help, places like Mission: Wolf can continue their efforts to ensure the gray wolf's greatest struggle for

survival is natural, not man-made. Please write Mission: Wolf at P.O. Box 211, Silver Cliff, CO 81249 or call (719) 746-2919.

 Mission: Wolf

NOW
DISAPPEARING
AT A LOCATION
NEAR YOU.

Can you picture a wolf in your mind? Well, soon that may be the only way to see one. But thanks to places like Mission:Wolf,

gray wolves have a 150 acre refuge to roam free of persecution and danger. And with your help, they can continue to appear in the

wild. Rather than in ads like these. Please write Mission: Wolf at P.O. Box 211, Silver Cliff, CO 81249 or call (719) 746-2919.

 Mission: Wolf

BRUTAL. SAVAGE.
COLD-BLOODED KILLERS.

BUT ENOUGH ABOUT US.

We have shot them from helicopters. Killed them in steel-clawed traps. We've poisoned them, beheaded them and sold their pelts

for financial gain. The time has come to help them. Because their survival is now our responsibility. For it is we who have jeopardized

their existence in the first place. Please write Mission: Wolf at P.O. Box 211, Silver Cliff, CO 81249 or call (719) 746-2919.

Mission: Wolf

(this page)
Agency: Fitzgerald + CO
Creative Directors:
Jim Paddock, Eddie Snyder
Art Director: Eddie Snyder
Designer: Monica McLeod

Copywriter: Jim Paddock
Photographer: Parish Kohanim
Director of Print
Production: Kathy Hoerler
Client: National Black
Arts Festival

(opposite)
Agency: Pollak Levitt & Nel
Creative Director: André Nel
Art Director: Brad Ramsey

Copywriter: Jeff Cole
Illustrator: Lee Land, Retouch
Photographer: Bryan Morehead
Client: Georgia Heritage Association

BUTTERWORT, *Pinguicula primuliflora*

IF ONLY THEY COULD ASK FOR THEMSELVES.
Join the voice of Georgia's endangered species and their natural habitats.
Call 1.888.948.2092. Because the longer you wait, the more the problem grows.

GEORGIA HERITAGE ASSOCIATION

GOPHER TORTOISE, *Gopherus polyphemus*

PLEASE GIVE

IF ONLY THEY COULD ASK FOR THEMSELVES.
Georgia's endangered species don't need handouts. But they do need shelter.
Call 1.888.948.2092. And help preserve what natural habitats are still left.

GEORGIA HERITAGE ASSOCIATION

FIVE-LINED SKINK, *Eumeces fasciatus*

IF ONLY THEY COULD ASK FOR THEMSELVES.
Please help save Georgia's endangered species and their natural habitats.
Call 1.888.948.2092. Because like it or not, you're the life preserver.

GEORGIA HERITAGE ASSOCIATION

(this page)
Agency: Asher & Partners
Creative Director: Bruce Dundore
Designer: Nancy Steinman
Copywriter: Jeff Bossin
Photographer: Myron Beck
Typography: Nels Dielman
Client: California Department of
Health Services

(opposite)
Agency: FGI
Creative Director: Denzil Strickland
Art Director: Rick Kourchenko
Copywriters: Rick Kourchenko,
Dennis Wipper
Photographer: Kelli Coggins
Client: Durham Literacy Council

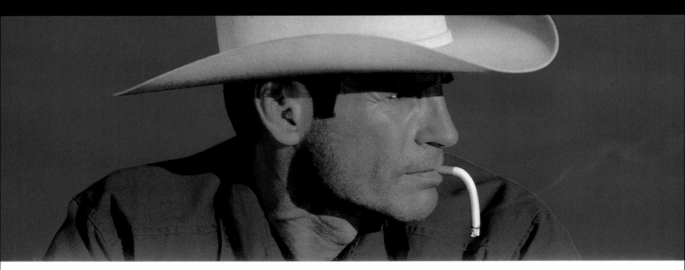

WARNING: SMOKING CAUSES IMPOTENCE

PROUD DAUGHTER
OF A DAD WHO
JUST LEARNED TO READ

MY MOM IS
A TERRIFIC STUDENT.
SHE'S LEARNING TO READ.

LET ME TELL YOU
ABOUT MY GRANDFATHER.
HE JUST READ HIS FIRST BOOK.

(this page)
Agency: Lowe & Partners/Monsoon
Creative Director: Khee Jin Ng
Art Directors:
Candy Kang, Thomas Yang
Copywriter: Rachel Goh
Photographer: Dong, Test Shot Studio
Client: Association of Women
For Action & Research

If he has broken more than your heart, don't suffer in silence. If you're willing to talk, an AWARE helpliner is here to listen. Call **1800-774 5935**, Monday to Friday, 4pm to 10pm. **aware**

(opposite)
Agency: Salles DMB&B
Creative Director: Mauro Salles
Designer: Daniel Venticinque
Copywriter: Marcelo Arbex
Photographer:
Ricardo de Vicq de Cumptich
Client: Radio, 9 De Julho

EM
1973
CALARAM
A
VOZ
DA
IGREJA.

Ajude a Rádio 9 de Julho da Arquidiocese de São Paulo a falar novamente.
Ligue 0900-782851 para doar R$ 10,00 ou deposite sua contribuição na conta
nº 53500-1 agência 614 do Banco Bradesco. Rádio 9 de Julho. Todo santo ajuda.

Rádio 9 de Julho
AM 1600 kHz

EM
1973
CALARAM
A
VOZ
DA
IGREJA.

Ajude a Rádio 9 de Julho da Arquidiocese de São Paulo a falar novamente.
Ligue 0900-782851 para doar R$ 10,00 ou deposite sua contribuição na conta
nº 53500-1 agência 614 do Banco Bradesco. Rádio 9 de Julho. Todo santo ajuda.

Rádio 9 de Julho
AM 1600 kHz

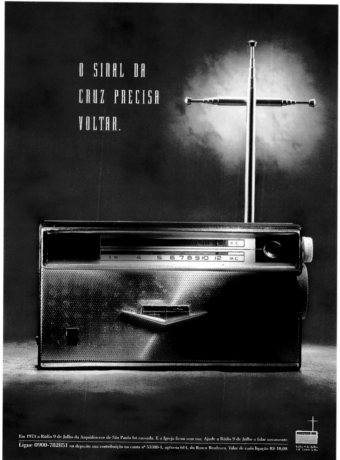

O SINAL DA
CRUZ PRECISA
VOLTAR.

Em 1973 a Rádio 9 de Julho da Arquidiocese de São Paulo foi cassada. E a Igreja ficou sem voz. Ajude a Rádio 9 de Julho a falar novamente.
Ligue 0900-782851 ou deposite sua contribuição na conta nº 53500-1, agência 614, do Banco Bradesco. Valor de cada ligação R$ 10,00.

Rádio 9 de Julho
AM 1600 kHz

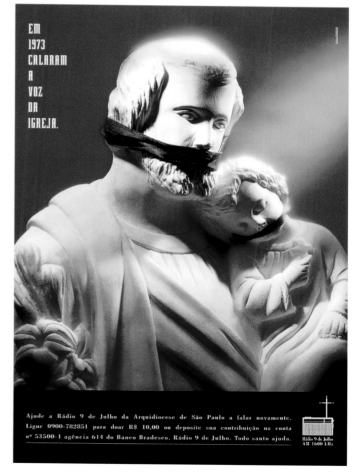

EM
1973
CALARAM
A
VOZ
DA
IGREJA.

Ajude a Rádio 9 de Julho da Arquidiocese de São Paulo a falar novamente.
Ligue 0900-782851 para doar R$ 10,00 ou deposite sua contribuição na conta
nº 53500-1 agência 614 do Banco Bradesco. Rádio 9 de Julho. Todo santo ajuda.

Rádio 9 de Julho
AM 1600 kHz

(opposite)
Agency: Ingalls
Creative
Director:
Rob Rich,
Steve
Bautista
Art Director:
Rob Rich
Copywriter:
Steve
Bautista
Sculptor:
Jeff Smith
Client:
Albany Times
Union

UN-Resolution? Sadomaso? Asthma?

Asien? Regenwald? Witwenverbrennung?

Ozonloch? Träume? Wetterbericht?

Afrika? Boxen? Ausländerhaß?

(this page)
Agency:
Heye + Partner
GmbH
Creative
Directors:
Peter
Hirrlinger,
Norbert
Herold,
Ralph
Taubenberger
Art Directors:
Ralph
Taubenberger,
Beate
Gronemann
Copywriters:
Peter
Hirrlinger,
Otward
Buchner,
Doris
Haider,
Sabine Richter
Client:
Süddeutsche
Zeitung

Grippewelle? Designerdroge? Cruise Missile?

Euro? Staatsbegräbnis? Buntwäsche?

Steve Silver, Curtis Melville
Art Director: Aaron Allen
Copywriter: David Knox
Client: San Jose Mercury News

TODAY SOMEONE WILL
WAKE DREAM REMEMBER
JOKE HACK CALL PRESUME
RESTRUCTURE MONOPOLIZE
DO FIND SURF PRAY WISH
PRACTICE LEVITATE CURSE
KNOW SWIVEL HOPE TAKE
WINCE CRY SMILE LAUGH
HOP TRIP CON HELP GULP
CAST SIP TURN REDO MOVE
STAY FUME ESTIMATE SETTLE
SCREAM MURDER SQUEEZE
OPEN TIPTOE REALIZE SENSE
ENJOY TELL OBSESS WEEP
THINK WANT LEAD KISS HEAL
REGROUP SEE DOUBT LIKE
SELL FIX CATER CARRY SCAN
ENVISION LEAVE ACT CLOSE
DEBUG TASTE DRINK SHOOT
NETWORK STEAL INTERVENE
CREATE INVENT PLAY LOVE
BREAK SOAR SAY CONTEND
BET SAVE ENDURE AWARD
COST LIMIT EXAMINE FAX
PARTY PLACE LUST ANALYZE
GROW WORK HUG INCREASE
FLOP LOOK STAR CARESS
PRAISE PAMPER CULTIVATE
RELISH HUMILIATE EMPATHIZE
DIGEST SHARE SLIDE ASK
SCRATCH SUPPORT FLOSS
SUBSIDIZE BATHE HUMOR
STIMULATE OVERHAUL GRIN
APOLOGIZE CONSOLE PURR
CODDLE TANTALIZE EXCITE
PACIFY PROTECT ZAP SCOUT
PHONE CORRESPOND SKID
NUZZLE DUEL HIDE TOAST
FORGIVE RETURN SACRIFICE
ACCESSORIZE LUG BESEECH
CRAVE CHARM FASCINATE
DRAG CRAWL WIN SPACKLE
OBLIGE PRETEND CONDENSE
ACQUIESCE SCARE ATTEND
NIBBLE KILL IMPLORE BAWL
SHOWER DRY SHAVE TRUST
GROVEL IGNORE DEFEND
COAX CLOTHE BRAG FUSE
FIZZ RATIONALIZE DETOXIFY
SANCTIFY GOLF GO POLISH
UPGRADE SPOIL EMBRACE
ACCEPT DESECRATE RESELL
JUDGE REFORM JITTERBUG
NURSE RESUSCITATE REPAIR
RESPECT ENTERTAIN CALM
DOWNSIZE PROFIT PROMISE
DELIVER TEASE FLIRT COMMIT
ECONOMIZE PERSIST DROP
SNUGGLE SCHMOOZE BITE
ELEVATE TOPPLE BOOGIE
NEGOTIATE SERVE HUMIDIFY
SOLVE GRATIFY PART CLICK
WALK PERSUADE FLIP CARE
SWING REBOOT SLIP TINGLE
SLAM-DUNK ROCK MANAGE
RUSH DRIBBLE DETERMINE
FINANCE KNEAD ENCHANT
AMAZE FOLD IDOLIZE SING
WORSHIP ARCH PAINT WAX
HURT INDULGE CLEAN CLIMB
COUNT INCLUDE ELIMINATE
OPERATE PROCESS REQUIRE
ALLOW DISCUSS PROVIDE
MODIFY TIP DEVELOP ISSUE
IDENTIFY FLAUNT DISSEMBLE
ADD RELEASE DANCE EXIST
LAUNCH CONTAIN FOCUS
INFORM LITIGATE FRIGHTEN
CLONE SHOUT LEER LISTEN
LEARN DOWNLOAD TOUCH
REORGANIZE OWN MOURN
AMALGAMATE EQUIP FLUFF
NIP CHEW EMPOWER GRIEVE
EDUCATE TOSS APPRECIATE
REJECT RESEARCH PRANCE
ROLL ANTICIPATE ASSOCIATE
ALIENATE HESITATE NURTURE
FEED DECORATE POKE JAB
EMIT EVOKE CHERISH ADORE
ADMIRE NOURISH CONSPIRE
INFLUENCE DRAW WHIMPER
FANTASIZE SWEAT ACTUALIZE
SEQUESTER FIGHT POISON
SWINDLE DESIGN PITY FAIL
PAW FALTER STUMBLE PULL
PUSH CRUMBLE SUCCUMB
STRENGTHEN RUB WEAKEN
REPORT SURRENDER SUBMIT
FORMULATE CRIPPLE INJURE
STOP SKI TAILOR PIT AVOID
TRANSFORM ROB APPROACH
HONOR RECOGNIZE DAZZLE
SUBSIST BURDEN PET SCOFF
EXECUTE TICKLE JOLT SHOCK
TEMPT HORRIFY INTIMIDATE
CONTROL IMPRISON PATROL
CAPTURE CORNER CAPTIVATE
MANIPULATE TRAP INFURIATE
ENTICE FREE SEDUCE FLEE
IRRITATE FLATTER DISAPPEAR
IMITATE FINISH YEARN EDIT
CUT COMPUTE BUY INVEST
CONVERGE PAWN NAVIGATE
DEMAND REMINISCE SPUR
CONNECT SLUMBER BLUFF
TOIL EXHUME PASTE PITCH
REGARD FLATTEN CHAGRIN
ACCOUNT SPARK LURE FINE
MASK WHOOP PROPEL POP
DEVASTATE SHUCK PROFESS
MUDDLE EXEMPLIFY RELENT
RAMPAGE FILE PREMEDITATE
CHAIN DECOY RELINQUISH
HERALD OVERCOME LURK
OUTCAST ATTEMPT CHANCE
SPRAIN DEEPEN BLATHER
PROMPT HAGGLE OUTFIT
ACCUMULATE JAR INSTIGATE
CHANNEL FREAK BEFRIEND
STRIKE ADORN WED QUIP
PROMULGATE ADULTERATE
CONCEPTUALIZE FAMILIARIZE
DISTORT PROGRESS SNARE
LOUNGE SHUDDER PERMIT
DWELL DWARF BLINDFOLD
CHEAPEN SUBTRACT ELATE
IMPART STALK DYE SPARKLE
PIQUE RESENT EXASPERATE
GLOW SWAP DRUG MARVEL
STRAIGHTEN INTRIGUE HUSH
EXTOL PUBLICIZE STARTLE
SEETHE EXPECTORATE WASH
PACK PLUCK LUNGE SWIPE
CATCH SUBDUE SUE REEL
WEATHER ROAR PRECEDE
STAGGER PARADE TANGLE
DIGRESS RIVET SYNDICATE
STICK BEGUILE BORE STEAM
DEFECT ESCAPE SEGREGATE
OVERTURN REPULSE WILT
UPBRAID REIGN EXCHANGE
OCCUPY HIRE OUTSTRETCH
SENSATIONALIZE TYPE ORATE
SLOUCH WHEEDLE FURNISH
INSIST REBEL REJUVENATE
LAUNDER SWITCH SCATTER
EXIT PUNISH TRANSFIGURE
EXTRICATE BLUNDER RESCUE
SALVAGE ENGINEER MOLD
DEDUCT RESPOND YODEL
DIVE TRAIN JOCKEY STYLE
DECRY MARRY FILM GAZE
RUMINATE SPLICE GLAZE
SIPHON SHAPE STASH VIEW
CONTRIBUTE QUALIFY TAX
PREDETERMINE DOWNPLAY
FUND TRANSACT REFLECT
DICTATE REVEAL POUT STRIP
RETREAT EXUDE SOLICIT TIME
INSPIRE RECHARGE RESIGN
RELOAD SUPERVISE REMIT
LIBERATE INQUIRE PREVAIL
JUXTAPOSE WOUND REPEAL
BUDGET DISMISS ALLY SORT
STAPLE OVERRIDE CURE END
TERMINATE UNIFY NOMINATE
LANDSCAPE FLUNK SLITHER
UNEARTH UNLOAD EXPLAIN
EXACERBATE CRADLE BACK
MULL PARTNER VACATION
OPT RENT STRUGGLE BIKE
REPLACE DESERT UNRAVEL
ABUSE MISTREAT EXTORT
UTTER RAID DONATE CHANT
HYPOTHESIZE INTERNALIZE
DISGRACE FARM PERPETUATE
ENLIVEN EXPLODE PILLAGE
BAPTIZE CRITIQUE BELITTLE
REPRODUCE DOMESTICATE
MENTOR PERSPIRE STRESS
WASTE DREAD ATTRIBUTE
CONCEIVE POLICE CROON
FICTIONALIZE ROMANCE JOG
PERJURE EAVESDROP LOOT
QUIBBLE LIBEL TERRORIZE
UNLEASH STOCKPILE RELAX
BATTER TERRIFY REHEARSE
MISTRUST YAMMER BLUSH
OVERBURDEN JUGGLE DIE
CONCLUDE PURSUE REPEL
ANESTHETIZE FISH TAN SCAM
FUSS IMBIBE PARSE DETAIL
MINE TAPE DISOBEY SURFACE
EXPENSE CATEGORIZE CHIRP
SPECTATE SCRIBBLE FASTEN
GLORIFY BETROTH STIPULATE
FESTER EXPERIMENT STRIVE
SAUTE REDDEN STIR CLAP
RECONSTRUCT WALTZ TUCK
HARRY RAP CLOAK SCALE
DOUBLE-CROSS SQUANDER
DOTE QUIZ STUPEFY PUFF
STIGMATIZE TWO-STEP SEW
TENDERIZE SCALD REPLICATE
REPACKAGE AUTHENTICATE
ABBREVIATE FADE ZONE HATE
MEDICATE DETACH VANISH
COMPLETE CHAFF RESOLVE
TRANQUILIZE SYMBOLIZE RIB
MOCK RECONCILE SCAMP
KID UNDERSTAND QUESTION
FEEL LAUD GRAB FERTILIZE
JIVE FLUSH FUMBLE RELAPSE
ENVELOP FLUCTUATE HEAR
ERADICATE EXHAUST SNIFFLE
EMERGE SATIATE SLAP MOPE
EQUIVOCATE TICK CHASTISE
INFLAME ACQUIRE CONSUME
GAIN DEVOUR NAP INGEST
PURCHASE PARTAKE FEAST
FILL ALARM RESIST VICTIMIZE
SECLUDE ELECTRIFY CURTAIL
DEPART MEASURE DESTROY
GRAPPLE STRETCH CRACK
YAWN WAVER GAWK IMPEDE
PANT PICK AGE DEMO AWAKE
FOOL AFFIRM AGONIZE BEAT
BEND CLING DRIVE FORBID
EAT LEAP FREEZE FORGET
HAVE STAB SHED PROVE
GUARANTEE METAMORPHOSE
MEET OVERDO TIRE QUIT
SHAKE PUT CIRCULATE RISE
WAIT SPEAK BRAND SMELL
SPRING TEACH RAM SPELL
TEAR THROW UPSET WIND
WRITE SPLIT E-MAIL SPRAY
EXPLORE FACE CHARGE BEAR
SHOW EDITORIALIZE SOAK
ATTACK LIGHT BLAST QUIET
DIVIDE PRESS TIE PARALYZE
ABSCOND TRAVEL ANIMATE
NUMB FIRE REVOLUTIONIZE
RECRUIT CHOKE WALLOW
COVER REKINDLE BEG IGNITE
START GROOVE FANCY BASK
WAG SLASH KICK STING
BLINK FLOAT COMMUNICATE
MYSTIFY SKETCH CLUTCH
SEIZE STRUT CONTEMPLATE
TRANSFER SICKEN RADIATE
POUR SHINE BAKE OFFER
SUBSCRIBE SCOOP ASSUME
POSE ADOPT MIMIC BINGE
FLASH BURST GUIDE WARN
LOSE SCURRY LIE DISPLAY
SPLURGE NEUTER SWARM
STORE JUMP CROWD LIFT
BOOST RAPE FORGE ORBIT
BULLY COMPLAIN MOOCH
MUMBLE PAUSE HURRY MUG
BARGAIN FOIL SKIM SILENCE
SMOTHER FRUSTRATE JOIN
HOOK LIMP TRICK DECIDE
ENVY SHY FLEX CONFUSE
GROWL EYE INCORPORATE
RETIRE SCHEME SUBLIMATE
PONDER INTOXICATE REMAKE
PHOTOGRAPH PHILOSOPHIZE
SCHEDULE SPY USE DRIP
BELONG MUSE HYPNOTIZE
CHANGE COOK REGRESS
DISINTEGRATE LICK BUILD
SNIFF OPPRESS SEPARATE
SCRAPE PONTIFICATE HASH
VETO ASSIST MULTI-TASK
PARAPHRASE MENTION SPIT
FOREWARN CRAFT FINESSE
LAST MATERIALIZE BREATHE
COMMINGLE ABDICATE BARE
EXONERATE SOB BULLDOZE
BE ILLUSTRATE INCRIMINATE
EXTERMINATE TRAUMATIZE
BRACE ASSIGN SWALLOW
SAVOR MASSAGE BOTHER
UNDERPERFORM SERENADE
PLACATE COLOR SMOOCH
SPIN STROKE LATHER HOARD
BELIEVE ARGUE CHALLENGE
CLASH HARPOON ADVANCE
BID ABANDON CONFIGURE
ALLAY IMPLEMENT IMPACT
CONCEDE MULTIPLY ATTACH
CLUSTER QUOTE APPLAUD
EVOLVE ARBITRATE POWER
ARTICULATE LOOM EMBED
MOUNT ABIDE MACHINATE
CRASH ABET ACCLIMATIZE
MAGNIFY APPEAR MALIGN
ABSOLVE CONCUR ABSORB
POWER-UP ABSTAIN GLISTEN
AVOW DIGITIZE CODE FAWN
UTILIZE DIRECT ACQUAINT
MERGE ACCUSE MELD BREW
ACQUIT GRASP FOG ADMIT
ADMONISH COLLIDE LIVE
FALL FORECAST COLLECT
COLLUDE CONFIDE MOLLIFY
FORTIFY FRAME OBSERVE
LEAN ASCRIBE BLACKLIST
PERSONIFY DEAL UPDATE
PROPOSE ACCREDIT AMEND
OBJECT REPRESENT RISK
VENTURE LOBBY COMFORT
BROWSE EXHALE ATTRACT
KIDNAP BUOY EXPERIENCE
BLACKBALL BUMP EXPEDITE
EXPECT BULGE CALCULATE
ELECT REPRIMAND TRACK
PRODUCE WATER FABRICATE
LICENSE CLOCK FOREBODE
BEGRUDGE DEBATE BRIDLE
APPOINT PROOFREAD JELL
VIDEOTAPE ACHIEVE RIVAL
LEGISLATE FLAY REPUDIATE
THREATEN BIFURCATE BUNDLE
CHOOSE WELCOME NAG
MELLOW BADGER DEMOTE
FEND REASON CASTIGATE
OVERRUN DISCLOSE DELETE
INVESTIGATE RECIPROCATE
RECOVER WOO CIRCUMVENT
BOMBARD DART CONQUER
RECOUP SPECULATE VALUE
CONSULT CRUMPLE RECITE
DEFEAT STAMMER MATURE
TRADE CUSTOMIZE RETRACT
REGURGITATE CHEAT FATHER
DENOUNCE EMBODY CAUSE
CHIME POLLUTE DISAPPOINT
ILLUMINATE HARASS OOZE
TATTOO VALIDATE SKYDIVE
BLAB ENCOURAGE DROOL
EXCLAIM WATCH HOB-NOB
DESIRE EXPOSE CO-DEPEND
SPONSOR DAYDREAM TYPIFY
ADVERTISE COMPROMISE
DETECT PATRONIZE BENEFIT
BURY CONTAMINATE DELAY
CATERWAUL DELIGHT DATE
EXERCISE FAVOR CENSOR
RETAIN INTERJECT CHUCKLE
MEDITATE CONVEY CORRODE
COUNSEL EXTINGUISH FAZE
MISREPRESENT COUNTERFEIT
CORRUPT COURT FALSIFY
AUTHORIZE FEAR CONFRONT
UNDERESTIMATE INACTIVATE
FINAGLE FATHOM CRUSH
ACCOMPANY TELECOMMUTE
CAMOUFLAGE FREELOAD
ONE-UP LURCH HARANGUE
OBTAIN EMPLOY GATHER
DISPARAGE IMPRINT INCITE
OPPOSE FRISK LUMP FROLIC
BOUNCE GOVERN LAG GRIP
GLOWER INCLINE PARROT
LANGUISH ACHE DEBILITATE
MANGLE ENRICH MASTICATE
AFFLICT DETONATE AFFIX
GAPE ENDOW BAN ENRAGE
ENGRAVE FLAP ENGULF LIST
ANCHOR AFFORD LENGTHEN
LAPSE DARE GUESS PRINT
HYPERLINK DEFER UNCOVER
DROWN FLOURISH LINGER
LULL SEARCH LOITER DEFILE
OBSCURE LOAN SEEK AIM
LOOSEN BROADEN AFFILIATE
CHARTER DEFY INTEGRATE
RAGE AID SQUIRM AFFRONT
BROACH ENHANCE ALIGN
AUTOMATE LINK ARCHIVE
AGGREGATE CHAT ALLOCATE
CHECKMATE ZIP CONCEAL
CONSTRUCT ACKNOWLEDGE
CENTRALIZE ACCESS DEPLOY
DISCOVER SCRIPT QUERY
ABATE PRIORITIZE ACCLAIM
STUFF DISENGAGE BRING
COMPLICATE ENGAGE ALLOT
INSTALL DECLINE SUPPRESS
BROIL MAINTAIN DEMOLISH
INTERACT EXPAND SPEED
ASTONISH CONVERT DEFINE
ANNOY HALLUCINATE REST
COMPLIMENT EXPROPRIATE
CONTORT DESCEND EFFECT
NULLIFY ANTECEDE SIGNAL
ASSORT BROOD AMPLIFY
ALERT BIND ANNEX INDICT
DESPISE INSTRUCT ECLIPSE
DENY ENROLL AVENGE CUFF
AUTOGRAPH RELY BALANCE
CUSS GAMBLE ENTRANCE
DABBLE NEUTRALIZE DALLY
DAMAGE ENTWINE EQUATE
MURMUR NARRATE MUSTER
CRIMP ESTRANGE CREEP
NEGATE ERR NOD ERASE
ESCHEW CLARIFY ESCORT
ESPOUSE FILCH EXCULPATE
CLENCH EULOGIZE ADDLE
EXULT MIRROR FACILITATE
ADAPT BLOOM ADJOIN CLIP
LEASE ADJOURN CITE CLOG
ADMINISTER EXCLUDE FENCE
GARNER FARE BLASPHEME
BLISTER EVICT CLOCK FEIGN
IMPLY BOOMERANG WRAP
BRAISE MIGRATE OBSOLESCE
DEBUT MILITARIZE GRADUATE
MISCUE KOWTOW RESCIND
AWAIT DERIDE AMELIORATE
DEBUNK DECANT BESIEGE
SHOWCASE AD-LIB GLEAN
MASH AUGMENT DECEIVE
DECIPHER EMBARK GARDEN
DECLARE HECKLE DEDUCE
MALTREAT DIVORCE FLAME
ICE EXHILARATE DISSOCIATE
BEWITCH RESEMBLE COIL
ASSUAGE COLLAPSE APPLY
COMBUST FIZZLE ADDRESS
REBOUND JUMBLE FROWN
DOODLE ENCOMPASS JINX
ESTABLISH TIGHTEN BUMBLE
POUND ASCEND SURPRISE
FLINCH AMUSE FLOUNDER
COLLATE REVIEW CRACKLE
FLOW ITEMIZE CHAFE SHUN
APPEAL COVET AGGRAVATE
FLOG SPRINT CREASE REVILE
CREDIT BEWILDER CRITICIZE
MARCH IMPLANT MARSHAL
HUNKER MARKET ASSESS
HANKER CARVE LODGE HEX
COMPETE SALIVATE BAFFLE
CONTRIVE HATCH BICKER
BARK HAUNT FAKE NITPICK
ACTIVATE DRESS HIGHLIGHT
BOIL ENDORSE MIX HOGTIE
CAPITALIZE ITCH PENETRATE
HOLLER EXTEND PHILANDER
HITCH PANIC BOND CANCEL
IDLE PERCOLATE PAR OUTDO
JOURNEY INDUCE ATROPHY
OVEREXTEND INFER AGITATE
INDUCT INJECT JEER SASS
CONJECTURE ANNUNCIATE
CONJUGATE RACE CONJURE
MEDIATE MODERNIZE ARRIVE
CONNIVE CONSENT HASSLE
BETRAY IRON FAINT SWELL
BLOW-DRY ADJUST JUBILATE
KEEN LABEL IRK KEEP LACK
TREMBLE MOISTEN FIGURE
LOWER RUIN INVADE INVITE
JAIL ENERGIZE MOSEY HEW
MUFFLE NOTIFY FERMENT
NUDGE OBLITERATE BLOCK
UNDERTAKE ERUPT OVEREAT
TRIM IMPLICATE DARN FIB
TRIUMPH INITIATE JUSTIFY
CONDEMN HINT MOTHER
REMIND REJOICE REWIND
INVOKE INTERFACE PLEDGE
PLAN REPEAT COLLABORATE
CRUNCH PROGRAM SIGH
INTERPRET PENALIZE BEGIN
WITHDRAW ENTRAP DEFORM
SCUFFLE JABBER STORM
MAGNETIZE HICCUP BLEED
WADDLE FORESTALL BRAID
REPROGRAM ASSURE SIGN
FOLLOW BACKLOG SLICE
TRANSCEND EXTEMPORIZE
RECONSIDER ASSASSINATE
OVERWHELM COORDINATE
ELUCIDATE SLURP PERFORM
UNCLASP WONDER ORDER
IMPROVISE TEST SECURE
COMMEMORATE TRADEMARK
COOPERATE TRIGGER LOAD
SUSPEND ANNOUNCE LOG
REQUEST BOOT CAMPAIGN
BROADCAST MEMORIALIZE
FINALIZE CACHE CATALOG
STUN COMPRESS OUTPUT
DECOMPRESS DEREGULATE
DEFAULT ENCODE FORMAT
RESTART AFFECT RETRIEVE
REGULATE OUTLINE REVAMP
FUEL CONTINUE RELOCATE
REDRESS PAY UNDERWRITE
ENCRYPT SERVICE DEPRIVE
LEVERAGE PROVOKE SPOOL
IMPOSE RHAPSODIZE PESTER
FEATURE UNVEIL COMPOSE
UNDERGO TESTIFY TABULATE
UPLOAD STRATEGIZE LEND
CONTRACT STAKE SNORKEL
INDEX ENCLOSE GENERATE
INDEMNIFY HUNT BOLSTER
CONSOLIDATE STRUCTURE
SURVEY COMPARE APPROVE
FREQUENT SPEND PREDICT
NOTE RAPPEL REINFORCE
ADVISE NECESSITATE GRANT
INTERVIEW CONSIDER SLAY
SATISFY BESTOW SUNBATHE
CAUTION RIDICULE PRESIDE
INSINUATE URGE TREASURE
DEVIATE OUTWIT TORTURE
MASTER OFFEND MANEUVER
MINIMIZE SHAME COMMAND
ENFORCE PERTURB PEAK
IMPERSONATE SULK PERFECT
PERUSE PETITION SUCCEED
REPRESS ASPIRE PORTRAY
INHERIT BABBLE CHALLENGE
TOP EVANGELIZE RETALIATE
DEMILITARIZE ABRADE ATTAIN
RESIDE REBUFF VERIFY HONK
CACKLE RECLINE CHORTLE
BRAINSTORM OUTPERFORM
DISRESPECT STUTTER INHIBIT
JOSTLE CHECK LEVEL PEEK
SUPPLANT ENABLE COERCE
WRECK SIZZLE CAUTERIZE
CHEER SEND HARMONIZE
IMAGINE REACH VOTE READ.

[DON'T BLINK]

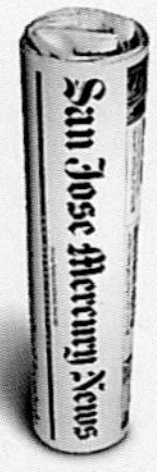

The Newspaper of Silicon Valley
800-870-NEWS

Agency: The Martin Agency
Creative Directors:
Kerry Feuerman, Joe Alexander
Art Director: Sean Riley
Copywriters:
Joe Alexander, Christopher Gyorgy,
Jonathan Mackler
Photographer: Craig Cameron Olsen
Studio Artist: Mark Brye
Print Producer: Edith Arbuckle
Client: Men's Health

(opposite)
Agency: Lowe & Partners/Monsoon
Creative Director: Khee Jin Ng
Art Directors:
Khee Jin Ng, Vincent Lee
Copywriter: Khee Jin Ng
Photographer: Alex Kaikeong,
Alex Kaikeong Studio

Clearer views.

Feed your mind.

Reader #21,591,671: Gets it to stay on top of things.

Reader #57,324,672: Hid in the sand to get near the shoot. Last night. At low tide.

Reader #22,648,213: Grabs it on his way to work.

(opposite, top, bottom)
Agency: Fallon McElligott
Creative Directors:
David Lubars, Mike Lescarbeau
Art Director, Designer:
Dawn McCarthy
Copywriter: Allon Tatarka
Client: Sports Illustrated

(opposite, middle)
Agency: Fallon McElligott
Creative Directors:
David Lubars, Mike Lescarbeau
Art Director: Dawn McCarthy
Copywriter: Linda Birkenstock
Client: Sports Illustrated

Liston? Here was a heavyweight unloved in victory, a joke in defeat who had come to a tragic end. "I pretty much identify with that life," said Tyson.
·SI 1/5/98·

Sports Illustrated
The guts of the game.

(this page)
Agency: Fallon McElligott
Creative Directors:
David Lubars, Bill Westbrook
Art Director: Bob Barrie
Copywriter: Linda Birkenstock
Photographer: Ken Regan
Client: Sports Illustrated

(this page)
Agency: Ingalls
Creative Directors: Rob Rich,
Steve Bautista
Art Director: Steve Tom
Copywriter: Brian Hayes
Photographer: Sean Kernan
Client: Boston Phoenix

If you think it's disturbing to find this in the newspaper,
imagine waking up to it on your front lawn.

This is not a pretty picture. But because Martin Luther King, Jr. would not tolerate this type of
hatred and injustice in his day, today we all wake up in a better world.

Phœnix

(opposite)
Agency: Fallon McElligott
Creative Director: David Lubars
Art Director: Bob Barrie
Copywriter: Dean Buckhorn
Client: Time Magazine

If there's a story in there,

we'll find it.

The world's most interesting magazine.

Always the truth.

Occasionally, the awful truth.

The world's most interesting magazine.

Was it show biz?

Was it science?

Yes.

The world's most interesting magazine.

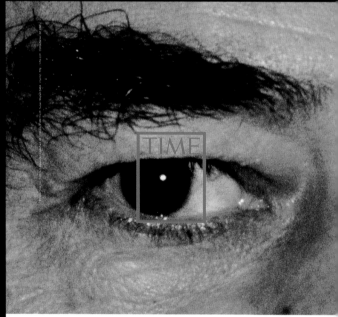

Iraq vs. the world.

Covered down to the last blink.

The world's most interesting magazine.

Creative Directors: Paul
Silverman, Steve Haesche
Art Directors: Michael
Ancevic, Steve Haesche
Copywriter: Bill Roden
Client: Newsedge

5:00 PM
News happens

5:00.07 PM
Sent to
desktops of
NewsEdge
subscribers

11:00 PM
Evening news

5:00 AM
Newspapers

11:30 AM
Weekly
magazines

12:00 PM
Monthly
magazines

6:00 AM
Talk radio

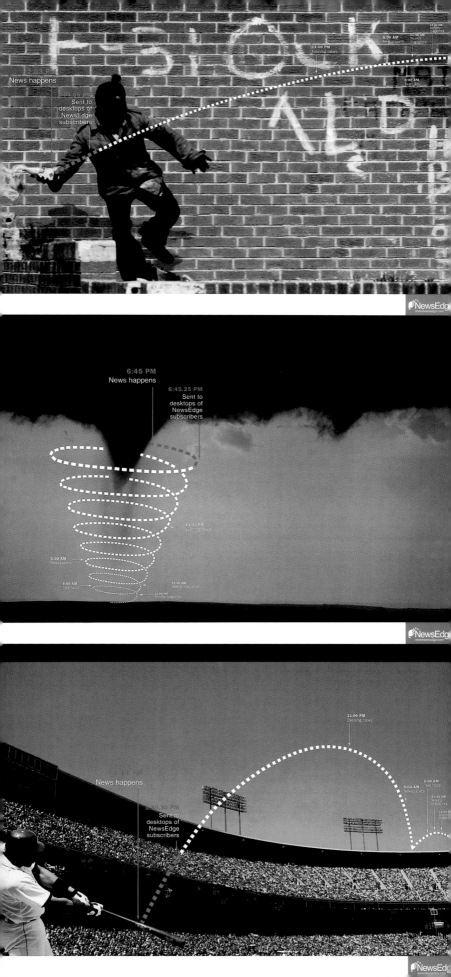

News happens
2:03 AM
Sent to
desktops of
NewsEdge
subscribers
5:00 AM
Newspapers
6:00 AM
Talk radio
11:00 PM
Evening news
11:35 PM
Weekly
magazines
12:00 PM
Monthly
magazines
NewsEdge
www.newsedge.com

6:45 PM
News happens
6:45.25 PM
Sent to
desktops of
NewsEdge
subscribers
11:00 PM
Evening news
5:00 AM
Newspapers
6:00 AM
Talk radio
11:30 PM
Weekly magazines
12:00 PM
Monthly magazines
NewsEdge
www.newsedge.com

11:00 PM
Evening news
News happens
3:27:30 PM
Sent to
desktops of
NewsEdge
subscribers
5:00 AM
Newspapers
6:00 AM
Talk radio
11:35 PM
Weekly
magazines
12:00 PM
Monthly
magazines
NewsEdge
www.newsedge.com

The Home Depot Invitational
We're very proud to support the spirit and competition of The Senior PGA Tour.

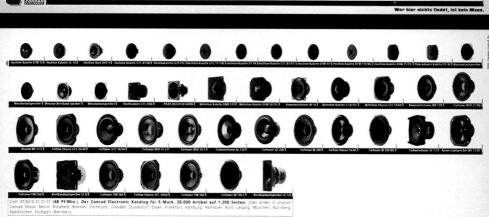
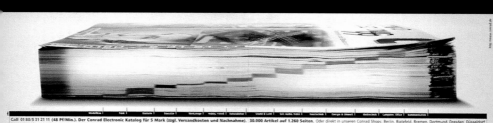

Agency: Fahlgren/Tampa
Creative Director: Scott Sheinberg
Art Director: John Stapleton
Copywriter: James Rosene
Client: Diamond Furniture Gallery

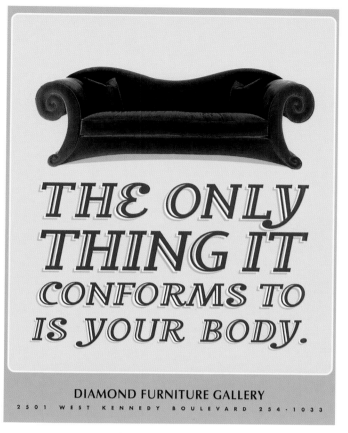

THE ONLY THING IT CONFORMS TO IS YOUR BODY.

DIAMOND FURNITURE GALLERY
2501 WEST KENNEDY BOULEVARD 254-1033

IT SAYS YOU'RE AN INDIVIDUAL. IT SAYS YOU'RE EXPRESSIVE. IT SAYS YOU'D ONLY ENTER AN ETHAN ALLEN TO USE THE BATHROOM.

DIAMOND FURNITURE GALLERY
2501 WEST KENNEDY BOULEVARD 254-1033

WHEN WAS THE LAST TIME THE CONVERSATION AROUND THE DINING ROOM TABLE WAS ABOUT THE DINING ROOM TABLE?

DIAMOND FURNITURE GALLERY
2501 WEST KENNEDY BOULEVARD 254-1033

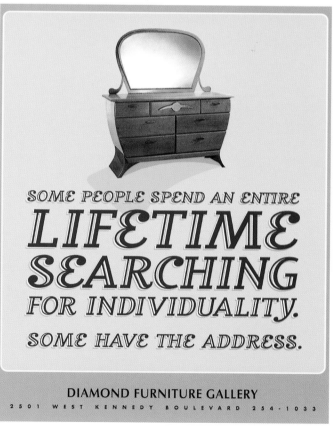

SOME PEOPLE SPEND AN ENTIRE LIFETIME SEARCHING FOR INDIVIDUALITY. SOME HAVE THE ADDRESS.

DIAMOND FURNITURE GALLERY
2501 WEST KENNEDY BOULEVARD 254-1033

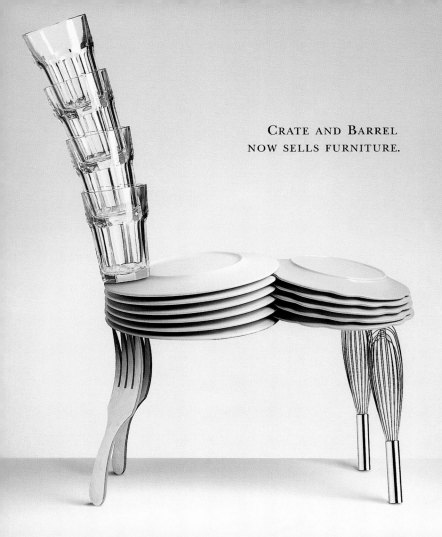

CRATE AND BARREL
NOW SELLS FURNITURE.

Crate&Barrel

The expanded Dallas Crate and Barrel opens Thursday, October 9, on the corner of Knox Street and McKinney.

(opposite)
(Agency: McConnaughy
Stein Schmidt Brown
Creative Directors:
Tom McConnaughy,
Jim Schmidt
Art Director, Designer:
Joe Stuart
Copywriter: Jim Schmidt
Photographer:
Francois Robért
Client: Crate and Barrel

The average person spends 26 years finding the right partner. 13 months finding the right church. 8 months finding the right caterer. And 6 months finding the right honeymoon spot. Which just may explain why the average person often ends up with the wrong plates.

Crate&Barrel

What does one of our tables have in common with an afternoon in the country? Or one of our chairs with a lakeside sunset? Well, all warmly embrace the concept of simplicity. Clearly a plus in a day and age when three-fourths of the world's surface is covered with water, but four-fifths is wired for cable.

Crate&Barrel

Crate&Barrel

It's the time of year when we raise a glass to our family and to our friends. To our pasts and to our futures. It's the time of year when we raise a glass to our dreams and to our hopes. In short, it's the time of year when there's a lot of pressure on a glass.

Crate&Barrel

Things were simpler "then." Or so we often hear. But if things were simpler "then," does that mean they have to be complicated now? Not by a long shot. At Crate and Barrel we've got a veritable store full of classic designs that prove "then" doesn't own simple. It merely has a timeshare.

(this page)
Agency: McConnaughy
Stein Schmidt Brown
Creative Directors:
Tom McConnaughy,
 Jim Schmidt
Art Director, Designer:
 Joe Stuart
Copywriter: Jim Schmidt
Photographers: Mark Laita,
Michael Kenna
Client: Crate and Barrel

(this page)
Agency: Heye + Partner GmbH
Creative Director: Norbert Herold
Art Director: Karlheinz Müller
Copywriters: Thorsten Meier,
Norbert Herold
Photographer: Christopher Thomas
Client: Alexa Montez

(opposite, top, bottom right)
Agency: Ingalls
Creative Directors: Rob Rich,
Steve Bautista
Art Director, Illustrator: Kathy Kuhn
Copywriter: Bruno Corbo
Photographer: Dan Nourie, Simko
Client: TJ Maxx

(opposite, bottom left)
Agency: Ingalls
Creative Directors: Rob Rich,
Steve Bautista
Art Director, Illustrator: Kathy Kuhn
Copywriter: Bob Fitzgerald
Photographer: Dan Nourie, Simko
Client: TJ Maxx

(this page)
Agency: Heye + Partner GmbH
Creative Director: Norbert Herold
Art Director: Karlheinz Müller
Copywriters: Thorsten Meier,
Norbert Herold
Photographer: Christopher Thomas
Client: Alexa Montez

Went to England   Went to Spain   Went to Malaysia   Got a frame
          Went to Brazil   Went to Uganda
                                              Took a trip to the maternity ward

POTTERYBARN

Late for Mother's Day brunch   Late for son's soccer game   Late for Thanksgiving dinner   Son asked if Santa's ever late
       Late for son's birthday party   Late for wedding anniversary   Late for son's Holiday pageant   Got a clock

POTTERYBARN

Got a job   Got a cube   Got an office   Got an office with a window   Quit to write a novel
                                        Got a bigger office   Got an office with a balcony   Got a desk

POTTERYBARN

(opposite)
Agency: Goodby, Silverstein
& Partners
Creative Directors: Rob Price,
Paul Curtin
Art Director, Designer:
Keith Anderson
Copywriter: Eric Osterhaus
Photographer: Bill Abronowicz
Print Producer: Hilary Read
Client: Pottery Barn

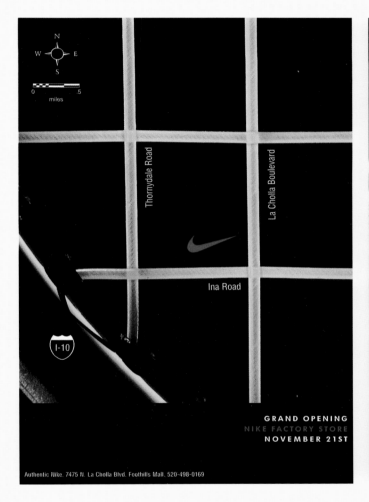

(this page)
Agency: Goodby, Silverstein
& Partners
Creative Director: Steve Simpson
Art Director: Joel Clement
Copywriter: Steve Zumwinkel
Photographer: Hunter Freeman
Client: Nike

(this page)
Agency: The Martin Agency
Creative Directors:
Hal Tench, Joe Alexander
Art Director: Sean Riley
Copywriter: Joe Alexander
Photographer: Hunter Freeman
Studio Artist: Dana Moses
Print Producer: Paul Martin
Client: Karsten
Manufacturing Corp. (Ping)

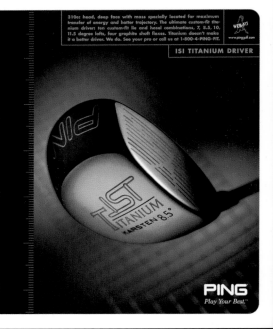

AND NOW,

FOR THE DISAPPEARING

BALL TRICK.

Soft, yet responsive feel, with the same impact force and distance control as our metal-faced putters. Perimeter-weighting, no-nonsense optics. Available in 6 popular models: Anser2i, Pal2i, ZING2i, Sedonai, B60i, B90i. After 45 majors and more than 1600 tour wins, we continue to chase perfection. See your pro or call 1-800-4-PING-FIT.

ISOPUR PUTTER SERIES

PING
Play Your Best.

HIT MORE FAIRWAYS. LESS CONDOS.

310cc head, deep face with mass specially located for maximum transfer of energy and hotter trajectory. The ultimate custom-fit titanium driver: ten custom-fit lie and hosel combinations, 7, 8.5, 10, 11.5 degree lofts, four graphite shaft flexes. Titanium doesn't make it a better driver. We do. See your pro or call us at 1-800-4-PING-FIT.

ISI TITANIUM DRIVER

PING
Play Your Best.

Agency: Goodby, Silverstein
& Partners
Creative Directors:
Jeffrey Goodby, Rich Silverstein
Art Director: Sean Farrell
Copywriter: Sharon Tao
Photographer: Heimo. Client: Nike

(this page)
Agency:
Goodby,
Silverstein
& Partners
Creative
Directors:
Jeffrey
Goodby,
Rich
Silverstein
Art Director:
Jon Soto
Copywriter:
Albert
Kelly
Photographer:
David
Maisel
Client: Nike

(opposite, top)
Agency:
Hammerquist
& Halverson
Creative
Director:
Fred
Hammerquist
Art Director,
Illustrator:
Matt
Peterson
Copywriter:
Ian Cohen
Photographer:
Natan
Bilow
Digital Artist:
Charlie
Rakatansky
Client: K2 Skis

(opposite, middle)
Agency:
Hammerquist
& Halverson
Creative
Director:
Fred
Hammerquist
Art Director,
Illustrator:
Matt
Peterson
Copywriter:
Ian Cohen
Photographer:
Scott
Markewitz
Digital Artist:
Charlie
Rakatansky
Client: K2 Skis

(opposite, bottom)
Agency:
Hammerquist
& Halverson
Creative
Director:
Fred
Hammerquist
Art Director,
Illustrator:
Matt
Peterson
Copywriter:
Ian Cohen
Digital Artist:
Charlie
Rakatansky
Client: K2 Skis

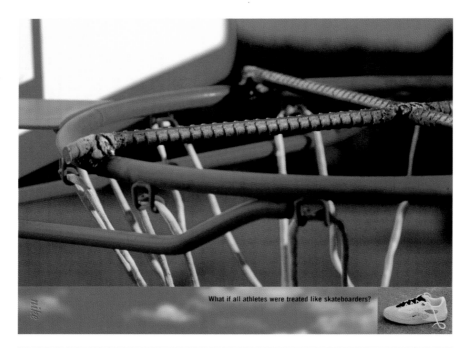

SWAMP BUGGIES. MILK CARTONS.

FUNNY CARS. MOTORCYCLES.

FROGS. HORSES. DOGS.

EACH OTHER. WE'LL RACE ANYTHING. ANYWHERE.

WHY? BECAUSE WE'RE AMERICAN AND WE RACE THINGS.

Smart Ski Technology.™ With this little red light you'll be sponsored by motor oil and detergent in no time.

THE MERLIN VI gives you, through SMART SKI TECHNOLOGY, the advantage to blast your way down the mountain with dampening high-speed vibration and maintaining control in and out of the turn. Because of its patented "Smart Structure" 90%. Because YOU ARE AN AMERICAN AND THESE ARE YOUR SKIS.

WE DIDN'T PICK SHRAPNEL OUT OF OUR BUTTOCKS JUST SO YOU COULD SIT YOUR LAZY ASS ON A CHAIR AND ONLY SKI THE GROOMED STUFF WE FOUGHT FOR YOUR FREEDOM AND WE'LL BE DAMNED IF YOU'RE NOT GOING TO USE IT.

Smart Ski Technology.™ This blinking red light will let you cover the mountain like a Green Beret.

THE NEW SHAPED X.15 gives you, through SMART SKI TECHNOLOGY, to rip the groomed or lure me steeps. The exclusive piezoelectric "Smart Structure" dampens high-speed vibrations and gives you control, so you can rip down anything you are on the mountain. YOU ARE AN AMERICAN AND THESE ARE YOUR SKIS.

IF BETSY ROSS WERE ALIVE

TODAY SHE'D SAY, "I LIKE

THAT YOUNG JONNY MOSELEY.

WHEN I'M DONE WITH THIS FLAG, I'M GONNA KNIT HIM

A SWEATER AND BAKE HIM A RHUBARB PIE."

Smart Ski Technology.™ This little red light makes you a better, faster American. God bless.

THE NEW SHAPED K2 FOUR gives you the freedom through SMART SKI TECHNOLOGY to hold speed the mountain bears that you may take before. Exclusive piezoelectric Smart Structure™ dampens high-speed vibrations. It allows you to maintain speed throughout the turns and keep control as you become a blur on the mountain. YOU ARE AN AMERICAN AND THESE ARE YOUR SKIS.

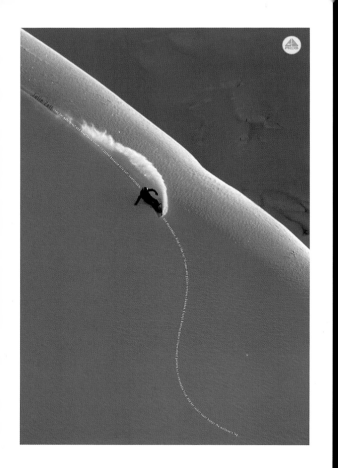

Rob Kingwill is warm, dry, and happy. he is warm and dry because his ACG jacket is waterproof and breathable. And he is happy because helicopters keep dropping him off on top of great big fluffy mountains just so he can ride down.

ACG

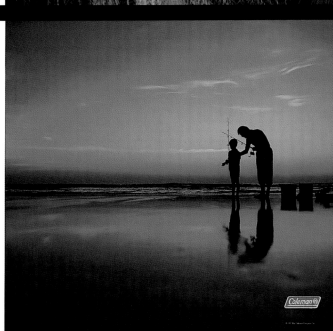

(opposite)
Agency:
Martin /
Williams
Creative
Director:
Lyle
Wedemeyer
Art
Director,
Designer:
Jim
Henderson
Copywriter:
Tom
Kelly
Photographers:
Brian
Bailey
(top),
Douglas
Walker
(middle),
Gary
Kufner
(bottom)
Product
Photographer:
Curtis
Johnson
Client: Coleman

(this page,
top, bottom)
Agency:
Goodby
Silverstein
& Partners
Creative
Directors:
Jeffrey
Goodby,
Rich
Silverstein
Art Directors:
Claude
Shade,
Keith
Anderson
Copywriter:
Steve
Simpson
Photographers:
Dave
McKenn,
Hans
Gissinger
Client: Nike

(this page,
middle)
Agency:
Goodby,
Silverstein
& Partners
Creative
Directors:
Jeffrey
Goodby,
Rich
Silverstein
Art Directors:
Claude
Shade,
Keith
Anderson
Copywriter:
Steve
Simpson
Photographers:
Dave
McKenn,
John Huet
Client: Nike

YOU ARE

Strapped To A Machine

and you sweat and groan and bruise and bleed.

If someone forced you to do it,

you would call it torture.

But you say: Strap me in, strap me tight, *this is fun.*

CAIRNS MTN. BIKING SHOE

nike ALPHA PROJECT

LOOK OUT, OR

You Are Toast.

The sun is firing its bright hot beams at your frail flammable skin.

It will burn parch scar broil roast you—and it always overcooks baseliners, always.

Do not be a *baseliner flambé.*

Refuse to be cooked.

CHALLENGE COURT DRI-FIT UV TOP

nike ALPHA PROJECT

See The Enemy.

Time is taunting you like a loudmouth jerk.

And the eyeball screams to the optic nerve which screams to the brain:

You are 7 seconds slower than you were yesterday.

You can't outrun Time, if you can't see Time.

TRIATHLON 350 RUNNING WATCH

nike ALPHA PROJECT

(this page)
Agency: Goodby, Silverstein
& Partners
Creative Directors:
Jeffrey Goodby, Rich Silverstein
Art Director: Steve Luker
Copywriter: Mark Fenske
Photographer: Nadav Kander
Client: Nike

(opposite)
Agency: Loeffler Ketchum Mountjoy
Creative Director:
Jim Mountjoy
Art Director: Doug Pedersen
Copywriter: Curtis Smith
Photographer: Pat Staub
Client: Nantahala Rafting

WATER MAY BE THE SOURCE OF ALL LIFE, BUT YOU'RE STILL REQUIRED TO SIGN A WAIVER.

THE RIVER IS A STICK. THE BOAT IS A PIÑATA. AND GOD ISN'T WEARING A BLINDFOLD.

THERE'S A REASON LIFE JACKETS ARE ORANGE. IT MAKES IT A LOT EASIER TO FIND THE BODIES.

THE DAY WE START SERVING
MARTINIS WILL BE OVER OUR DEAD BODIES.
Check in next week.

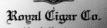

Royal Cigar Co.
Atlanta's oldest cigar store

HOW LONG HAVE WE BEEN
SELLING CIGARS IN ATLANTA? LET'S PUT IT THIS WAY:
Sherman came in here asking for a match.

Royal Cigar Co.
Atlanta's oldest cigar store

LIKE EVERYONE ELSE,
WE'RE TRYING TO CAPITALIZE ON THIS CIGAR CRAZE.
We just need to do it a lot faster.

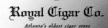

Royal Cigar Co.
Atlanta's oldest cigar store

(opposite)
Agency: FGI
Creative Director, Copywriter:
Denzil Strickland
Art Director: Jimmy Bonner
Photographer: Mark Gooch
Digital Artist: Richard Paschal
Client: Royal Cigar Co.

(this page)
Agency: Elgin/DDB
Creative Director: Marty McDonald
Art Director: Greg Braun
Copywriter: Chris Halas
Photographers: Mark Hooper,
Mel Curtis
Lettering Artist: Terisa Wingert
Client: Don Tomas Cigars

(left)
Agency: GSD&M
Creative Director: Brian Brooker
Art Director: Anne Stevenson
Copywriter: Todd Alley
Illustrator: Digitango
Print Producer: Leigh Ann Proctor
Client: Southwest Airlines

(right)
Agency: GSD&M
Creative Director, Copywriter:
Brian Brooker
Art Director: Holland Henton
Photographer: Jimmy Williams,
Jimmy Williams Productions
Print Producer: Leigh Ann Proctor
Client: Southwest Airlines

Southwest Airlines. The Official Airline Of The Texas Rangers.

(this page)
Agency: The Martin Agency
Creative Director,
Art Director: Hal Tench
Copywriter: Raymond McKinney
Photographers: Meredith
Parmelee, Tim Gabbert
Print Producer: Marge Hickman
Client: Marriott International, Inc.

(opposite)
Agency: Mullen
Creative Director, Copywriter:
Edward Boches
Art Director: Michael Ancevic
Photographer: Scott Goodwin
Client: New England Steamship
Foundation

don't sleep just anywhere

don't sleep just anywhere

Stay at a place you know you can count on. At Fairfield Inn® by Marriott, you always get a clean, comfortable room, free continental breakfast, a pool and smart, friendly service. All for

FAIRFIELD INN
by Marriott
You can expect more™

around $45-$65 a night? And since it's by Marriott, Marriott® Rewards™ members earn points toward a free vacation.

Call your travel agent or 800-228-2800. Or visit us at www.fairfieldinn.com.

Stay at a place you know you can count on. At Fairfield Inn® by Marriott, you always get a clean, comfortable room, free continental breakfast, a pool and smart, friendly service. All for

FAIRFIELD INN
by Marriott
You can expect more™

around $45-$65 a night? And since it's by Marriott, Marriott® Rewards™ members earn points toward a free vacation.

Call your travel agent or 800-228-2800. Or visit us at www.fairfieldinn.com.

How many fish will you catch?

Will you even make a cast?

On rivers like the Firehole, the Snake, the Green and the North Platte, catching a nice trout isn't exactly hard to do. Once you make a cast, that is. For when you see the beauty of these places, when you see water flowing past green, through valleys and down canyons, it can be easy to forget, for a few moments, that there's fishing to be done. For a free Vacation Guide, call 1-800-225-5996. Or visit us at www.wyomingtourism.org

WYOMING

Do you have a favorite color?

Do you still?

Looking out upon Yellowstone's Hayden Valley, upon the many shades of green and red and yellow and blue, it is hard to imagine how one could remain partial to a single color. The same could be said of Jenny Lake, the Wind River Range or the countless other places where there's a meeting of Wyoming's forests, meadows, mountains, water and sky. For a free Vacation Guide, call 1-800-225-5996. Or visit us at www.wyomingtourism.org

WYOMING

Ever dream of being a cowboy?

Want to see where you'd live?

It's a land of saddles and spurs and buckrail fences. Of Palominos and Paints and Sorrels. Of big skies, wide open spaces and mountain range after mountain range. And this land, it's not called your imagination. It's called Wyoming. It's called towns like Cody, Ten Sleep and Pinedale. Places like the Hole in the Wall. Things like trail rides and rodeos. For a free Vacation Guide, call 1-800-225-5996. Or visit us at www.wyomingtourism.org

WYOMING

(opposite)
Agency: Riddell Advertising & Design
Creative Director: Ed Riddell
Art Director: Dan Bryant
Copywriter: Jim Hagar
Photographer: Harry DeZitter
Client: Wyoming Tourism

We have no branches.

For an authentic tropical island holiday, there is only one destination: Mauritius.
Write in to MTIS, 2D, Phoenix Estate, 462 Tulsi Pipe Road, Mumbai-13. Tel: 4954854.

MAURITIUS
99% fun 1% land

Shaken.
Not stirred.

A typical racy, action-packed day in the tropical island of Mauritius. For information,
write in to MTIS, 2D, Phoenix Estate, 462 Tulsi Pipe Road, Mumbai-13. Tel: 4954854.

MAURITIUS
99% fun 1% land

(this page)
Agency: Trikaya Grey Advertising
India Ltd.
Creative Directors: Alok Nanda,
Kanad Banerjee
Art Director: Kanad Banerjee
Copywriter: Alok Nanda
Photographer: Prabuddha Das Gupta
Client: Mauritius Tourism
Information Service

(this page)
Agency: Young & Rubicam
Creative Director: Reid Miller
Art Director: Glen Stevens
Photographer: Craig Cutler
Client: United Airlines

(opposite)
Agency: Goodby, Silverstein & Partners
Creative Directors:
Jeffrey Goodby, Rich Silverstein
Art Director: Paul Hirsch
Copywriter: Josh Denberg
Photographer: Raymond Meeks
Client: Keystone Resort

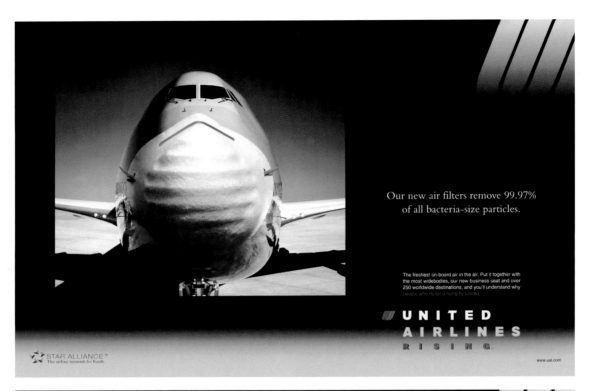

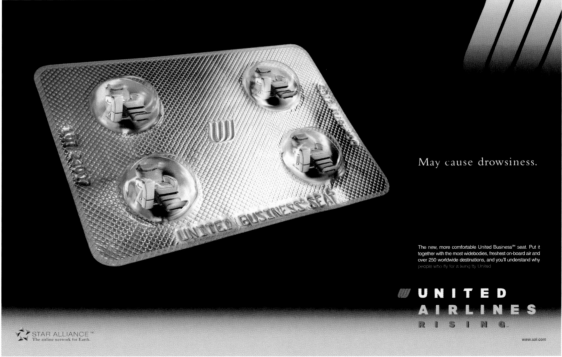

JUST WHEN YOU THOUGHT THE PLACE COULDN'T GET ANY PRETTIER, IT STARTS TO TURN COLORS.

WHEN YOU START WITH BEAUTY AND ADD STUNNING FALL COLORS, WHAT DO YOU GET?

ONLY THE MOST ENCHANTING, RELAXING AND VISUALLY SATISFYING GETAWAY YOU COULD EVER IMAGINE. TO HELP PLAN

YOUR GETAWAY, CALL THE WISCONSIN FALL HOTLINE AT 1-800-432-8747. **WISCONSIN**

(opposite)
Agency: Laughlin/Constable
Creative Director: Steve Laughlin
Art Director: Bill Kresse
Copywriter: Sheldon Rusch
Photographers:
Zane Williams, Scott Lanza
Client: Wisconsin Division of Tourism

(this page)
Agency: Publicis Werbeagentur Gmbh
Creative Directors:
Michael Köcher, Harald Schmitt
Art Directors: Harald Schmitt,
Katja Le Blond
Copywriter: Michael Köcher
Illustrator: Armin Popp. Client: Taxi

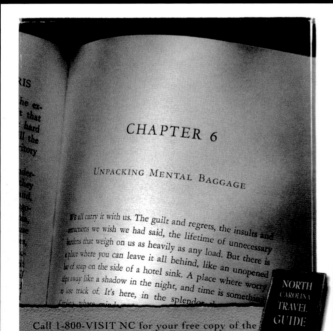

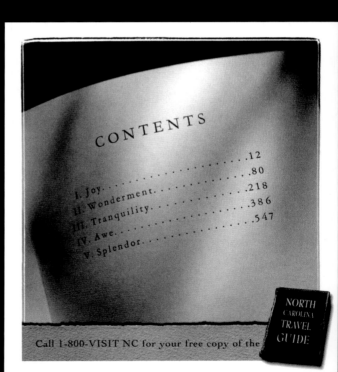

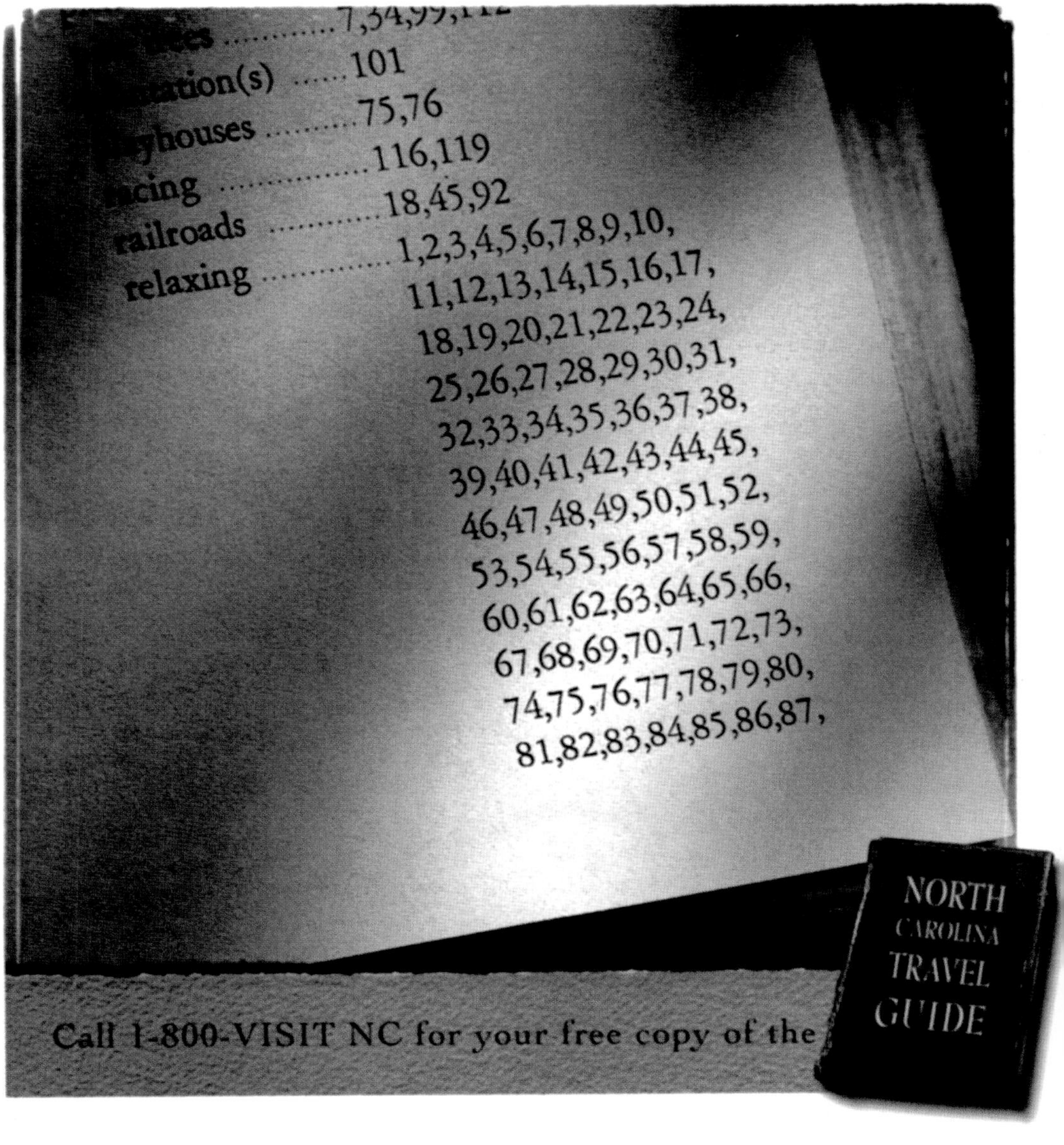
101
75,76
116,119
railroads 18,45,92
relaxing 1,2,3,4,5,6,7,8,9,10,
11,12,13,14,15,16,17,
18,19,20,21,22,23,24,
25,26,27,28,29,30,31,
32,33,34,35,36,37,38,
39,40,41,42,43,44,45,
46,47,48,49,50,51,52,
53,54,55,56,57,58,59,
60,61,62,63,64,65,66,
67,68,69,70,71,72,73,
74,75,76,77,78,79,80,
81,82,83,84,85,86,87,
Call 1-800-VISIT NC for your free copy of the
NORTH CAROLINA TRAVEL GUIDE

ꟻORMED FROM ENORMOUS AMOUNTS OF PRESSURE AND STRESS, THEY'VE BEEN RELIEVING THEM EVER SINCE.

1-800-VISIT NC
www.visitnc.com
NORTH CAROLINA

Ɪꟻ THE TIDE HAD ITS WAY, IT WOULD NEVER GO OUT.

1-800-VISIT NC
www.visitnc.com
NORTH CAROLINA

(opposite)
Agency: Loeffler Ketchum Mountjoy
Creative Director: Jim Mountjoy
Art Director: Doug Pedersen
Copywriter: Curtis Smith
Photographers: Kelly Culpepper *(top)*
Harry DeZitter *(bottom)*
Client: North Carolina Travel
& Tourism

(this page)
Agency: McConnaughy Stein
Schmidt Brown
Creative Director: Jim Schmidt
Art Director: Jon Wyville
Copywriter: Dave Loew
Client: Pub Tours of Ireland Ltd.

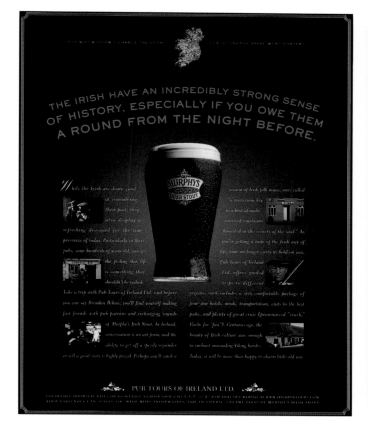

(opposite)
Agency: Publicis & Hal Riney
Executive Creative Directors:
John Doyle, Dave O'Hare
Art Director: John Doyle
Copywriter: Dave O'Hare
Photographer: R. J. Muna
Client: Aspen Skiing Company

There are over a hundred
restaurants and watering
holes between Aspen
and Snowmass, including one
just off the Big Burn,
where each day as the sun
takes its final bow along
Garrett's Peak, the beer,
for some inexplicable reason,
tastes better here.

Aspen.

There's a look your kids get when they
suddenly realize something. Something wondrous like
the door they just walked through to go to sleep tonight
is the same door they'll ski out of tomorrow morning.
You know that look, don't you? It comes easier here.

Snowmass Village at Aspen.

Whoever invented skiing should
be thanked, as often and
in as many ways as possible.
There are nearly three hundred
runs here, big enough for you to
express your gratitude, yet small
enough that your thanks will be
heard. Go ahead, offer one up.
It'll feel better here.

Aspen.

(this page)
Agency: Wongdoody
Creative Director: Tracy Wong
Art Directors, Designers:
Jason Black, Mark Watson
Copywriter: Jacket McCullough
Print Producer: Angie Schraw
Client: Alaska Airlines

(opposite)
Agency: Wongdoody
Creative Director: Tracy Wong
Art Director, Designer:
Jason Black
Copywriter: Jeanne Ivy
Print Producer: Angie Schraw
Client: Alaska Airlines

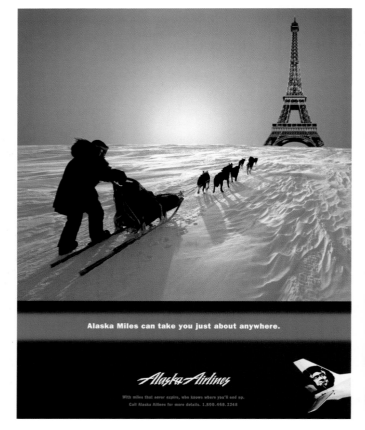

IndicesVerzeichnisIndex

Creative Directors Art Directors Designers

Agencies Clients

Copywriters Photographers Illustrators

Graphis Books Promotion

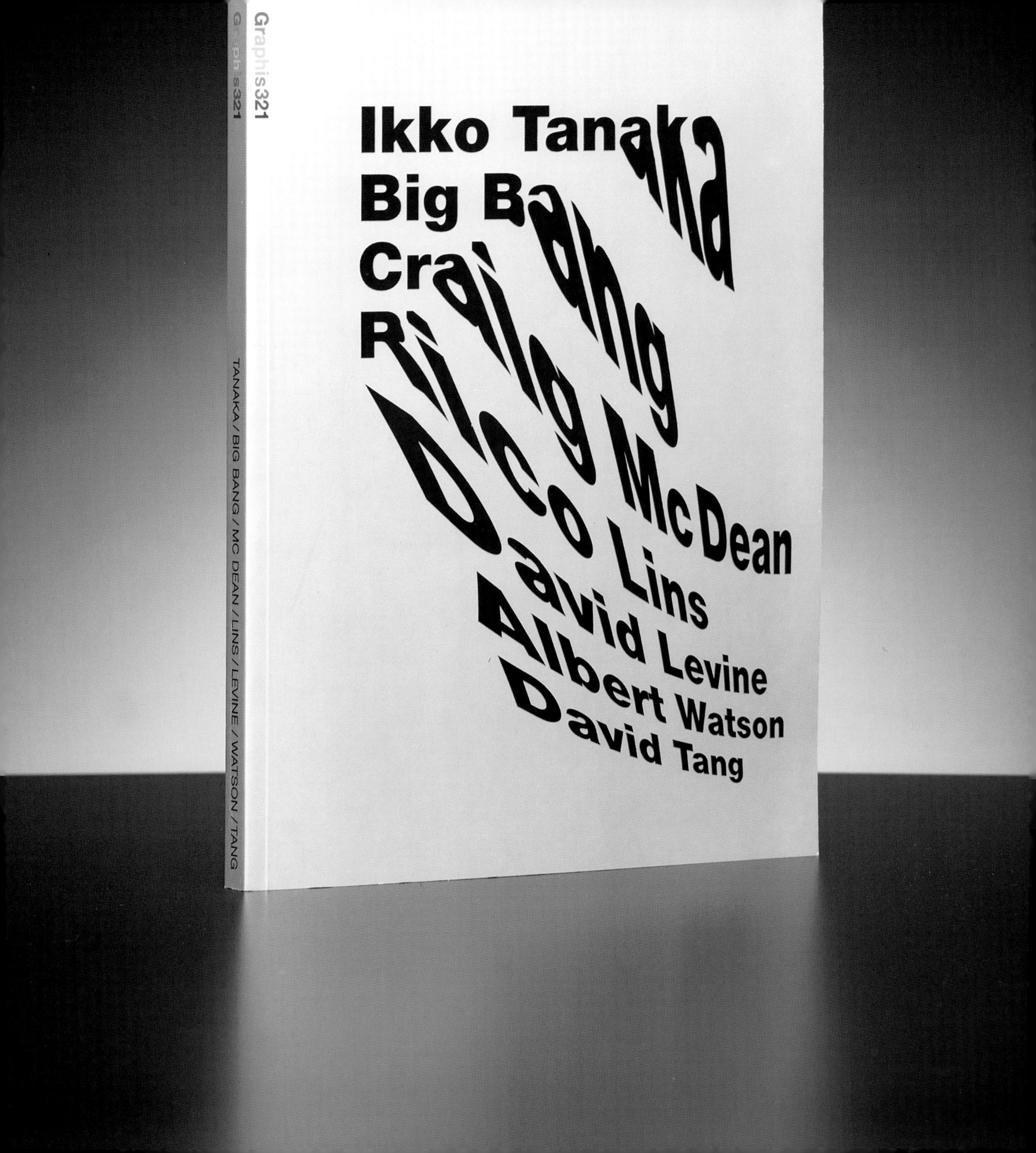

Ikko Tanaka
Big Bang
Craig
R
Deco McDean
co Lins
avid Levine
Albert Watson
David Tang

Order Form

We're introducing a great way to reward Graphis magazine readers: If you subscribe to Graphis, you'll qualify for a 40% discount on our books. If you subscribe and place a Standing Order, you'll get a 50% discount on our books. A Standing Order means we'll reserve your selected Graphis Annual or Series title(s) at press, and ship it to you at 50% discount. With a Standing Order for Design Annual 1999, for example, you'll receive this title at half off, and each coming year, we'll send you the newest Design Annual at this low price — an ideal way for the professional to keep informed, year after year. In addition to the titles here, we carry books in all communication disciplines, so call if there's another title we can get for you. Thank you for supporting Graphis.

Book title	Order No.	Retail	40% off Discount	standing order 50% off	Quantity	Totals
Advertising Annual 1999	1500	☐ $70.00	☐ $42.00	☐ $35.00		
Annual Reports 6 (s)	1550	☐ $70.00	☐ $42.00	☐ $35.00		
Apple Design	1259	☐ $45.00	☐ $27.00	N/A		
Black & White Blues	4710	☐ $40.00	☐ $24.00	N/A		
Book Design 2 (s)	1453	☐ $70.00	☐ $42.00	☐ $35.00		
Brochures 3 (s)	1496	☐ $70.00	☐ $42.00	☐ $35.00		
Corporate Identity 3 (s)	1437	☐ $70.00	☐ $42.00	☐ $35.00		
Digital Photo 1 (s)	1593	☐ $70.00	☐ $42.00	☐ $35.00		
Ferenc Berko	1445	☐ $60.00	☐ $36.00	N/A		
Information Architects	1380	☐ $35.00	☐ $21.00	N/A		
Interactive Design 1 (s)	1631	☐ $70.00	☐ $42.00	☐ $35.00		
Letterhead 4 (s)	1577	☐ $70.00	☐ $42.00	☐ $35.00		
Logo Design 4 (s)	1585	☐ $60.00	☐ $36.00	☐ $30.00		
New Talent Design Annual 1999	1607	☐ $60.00	☐ $36.00	☐ $30.00		
Nudes 1	212	☐ $50.00	☐ $30.00	N/A		
Photo Annual 1998	1461	☐ $70.00	☐ $42.00	☐ $35.00		
Pool Light	1470	☐ $70.00	☐ $42.00	N/A		
Poster Annual 1999	1623	☐ $70.00	☐ $42.00	☐ $35.00		
Product Design 2 (s)	1330	☐ $70.00	☐ $42.00	☐ $35.00		
Promotion Design 1 (s)	1615	☐ $70.00	☐ $42.00	☐ $35.00		
T-Shirt Design 2 (s)	1402	☐ $60.00	☐ $36.00	☐ $30.00		
Typography 2	1267	☐ $70.00	☐ $42.00	☐ $35.00		
Walter Iooss	1569	☐ $60.00	☐ $36.00	N/A		
World Trademarks	1070	☐ $250.00	☐ $150.00	N/A		

Shipping & handling per book, US $7.00, Canada $15.00, International $20.00.

New York State shipments add 8.25% tax.

Standing Orders I understand I am committing to the selected annuals and/or series and will be automatically charged for each new volume in forthcoming years, at 50% off. I must call and cancel my order when I am no longer interested in purchasing the book. (To honor your standing order discount you must sign below.)

Signature   Date

Graphis magazine	☐ One year subscription	USA $90	Canada $125	Int'l $125	
	☐ Two year subscription	USA $165	Canada $235	Int'l $235	
	☐ One year student*	USA $65	Canada $90	Int'l $90	
	☐ Single or Back Issues (per)	USA $24	Canada $28	Int'l $28	

*All students must mail a copy of student ID along with the order form.

(s) = series (published every 2-4 years)

Name	☐ American Express ☐ Visa ☐ Mastercard ☐ Check
Company	
Address	Card #
City State Zip	Expiration
Daytime phone	Card holder's signature

Send this order form (or copy) and make check payable to Graphis Inc. For even faster turn-around service, or if you have any questions about subscribing, call us at the following numbers: in the US (800) 209. 4234; outside the US (212) 532. 9387 ext. 242 or 240; fax (212) 696. 4242. Mailing address: Graphis, 141 Lexington Avenue, New York, New York 10016-8193. Order Graphis on the Web from anywhere in the world: .<www.graphis.com>.

Graphis Books Call For Entry

If you would like us to put you on our Call for Entries mailing list for any of our books, please fill out the form and check off the specific books of which you would like to be a part. We now consolidate our mailings twice a year for our spring and fall books. If information is needed on specific deadlines for any of our books, please consult our website: www.graphis.com.

Graphic Design Books
☐ Advertising Annual
☐ Annual Reports
☐ Book Design
☐ Brochure
☐ Corporate Identity
☐ Design Annual
☐ Digital Fonts
☐ Diagrams

☐ Poster Annual
☐ Products by Design
☐ Letterhead
☐ Logo Design
☐ Music CD
☐ New Media
☐ Packaging
☐ Paper Promotions
☐ Typography

Photography Books
☐ Digital Photo (Professional)
☐ Human Cond. (Photojournalism)
☐ New Talent (Amateur)
☐ Nudes (Professional)
☐ Nudes (Fine Art)
☐ Photo Annual (Professional)
☐ Photography (Fine Art)

Student Books
☐ Advertising Annual
☐ Design Annual
☐ Photo Annual (Professional)
☐ Products by Design
☐ All the Books
☐ All Design Books only
☐ All Photo Books only
☐ All Student Books only

First Name: _____ Last Name: _____

Company: _____

Telephone: _____ Fax: _____

Mailing Address: _____ City: _____

State, Country: _____ Zip: _____

Mail form or copy to: Graphis, Call for Entries, 141 Lexington Ave., New York, New York 10016-8139, USA, or fax to (212) 213. 3229.